PROBLEM SOLVING THROUGH

'C' PROGRAMMING

ASLAM J. KARJAGI

ISBN 979-888569123-9

I

DEDICATE

This Book

To

My beloved parents

For always supporting & loving me,

Students

I have known over the years, who have taught me humility & what it means to be a Teacher

&

To every teacher who loves to teach

Contents

Foreword

Problem Solving Through
C Programming
FIRST EDITION

Aslam. J. Karjagi B.E,M.Tech,(PhD)
Assistant Professor
Department of Computer Science & Engineering
Secab Institute of Engineering & Technology
Vijayapura, Karnataka

Publisher Name
MRK Publications
Ranjan Kumar Thapa, M.Sc, B.Ed
Office: Sainikpuri, khaprail Bazar,
PO New Chumta, PS Matigara
Distt.Darjelling, City: Siliguri(W.B)
Pin: 734009
Email: ranjanthapa316@gamil.com
Contact: 8116782587

Preface

Preface

C is a general-purpose programming language that is extremely popular, simple, and flexible to use. It is a structured programming language that is machine-independent and extensively used to write various applications, Operating Systems like Windows, and many other complex programs like Oracle database, Git, Python interpreter, and more. One can say, C is a base for the programming. If you know 'C,' you can easily grasp the knowledge of the other programming languages that uses the concept of 'C'

Learning C programming has lot of benefits, but the foremost thing in which it helps is to understand the underlying architecture of how things work. If a person learns C programming first, it will help him to learn any modern programming language as well.

This book is designed for practical C programming. C is currently the premier language for software developers. That's because it's widely distributed and standard. Newer languages are available, such as C++, but these are still evolving. C is still the language of choice for robust, portable programming. This book will help students to understand basics of C programming language, through easy to understand diagrams and real time examples. Simple programs are included for every concept with proper syntax and semantics.

This book will certainly help students to understand various concepts in simple and easy way thus making learning Simple & Easy.

It's my humble request to support for further improvement through your valuable suggestions and constructive comments.

E-mail: aslamkarjagi88@gmail.com

Contact: +91-9964157055, 7892529422

Aslam. J. Karjagi

Acknowledgements

First Edition: 2021

DISCLAIMER The publisher has put forth its best effort in preparing and arranging this book. The information provided herein by the author is presented "as-in". The publisher and author disclaim any liabilities in connection with the use of information presented in this book.

ISBN: 0000000355162 Publication By: MRK Publications

Printed and type set by: MRK Publications Distribution by: MRK Publications

CHAPTER ONE

Module-1 INTRODUCTIONTOCOMPUTERHARDWARE

1.1 Computer: Definition

A computer is a machine that can be programmed to manipulate symbols. Its principal characteristics are:

- It responds to a specific set of instructions in a well-defined manner.
- It can execute a pre-recorded list of instructions (a program).
- It can quickly store and retrieve large amounts of data.

Therefore computers can perform complex and repetitive procedures quickly, precisely and reliably. Modern computers are electronic and digital. The actual machinery (wires, transistors, and circuits) is called hardware; the instructions and data are called software. All general-purpose computers require the following hardware components:

- Central processingunit (CPU): The heart of the computer, this is the component that actually executes instructions organized in programs ("software") which tell the computer what to do.
- Memory (fast, expensive, short-term memory): Enables a computer to store, at least temporarily, data, programs, and intermediate results.
- Mass storage device (slower, cheaper, long-term memory): Allows a computer to permanently retain large amounts of data and programs between jobs. Common mass storage devices include disk drives and tape drives.
- Input device: Usually a keyboard and mouse, the input device is the conduit through which data and instructions enter a computer.
- Output device: A display screen, printer, or other device that lets you see what the computer has accomplished.

In addition to these components, many others make it possible for the basic components to work together efficiently. For example, every computer requires a bus that transmits data from one part of the computer to another.

1.2 Computer Generations:

The development of computer systems is normally discussed as the development over different generations. With the succession of different generations, came the advancement in computer technology.

1.21 First Generation

- The period 1940 to 1956, roughly considered as the First Generation of Computer.
- The first generation computers were developed by using vacuum tube or thermionic valve machine.
- The input of this system was based on punched cards and paper tape; however, the output was displayed on printouts.
- The first generation computers worked on binary-coded concept (i.e., language of 0& 1)

1).**Examples:** ENIAC, EDVAC, etc.

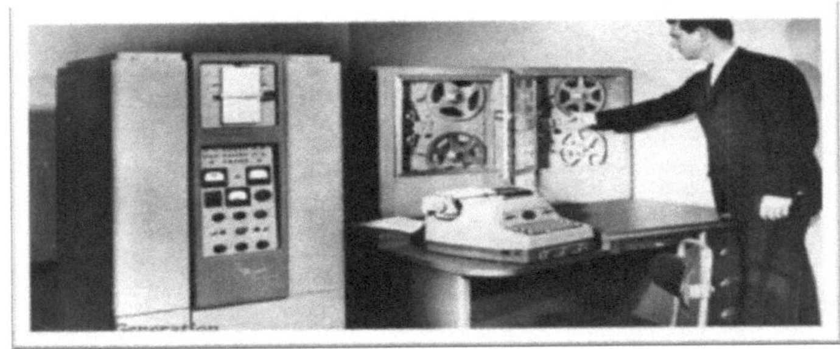

Fig 1.21: First Generation Computer

1.22 Second Generation

- The period 1956 to 1963 is roughly considered as the period of Second Generation of Computers.
- The second generation computers were developed by using transistor technology.
- In comparison to the first generation, the size of second generation was smaller.
- In comparison to computers of the first generation, the computing time taken by the computers of the second generation was lesser**ig 1.22: Second Generation Computer**

1.23 Third Generation

- The period 1963 to 1971 is roughly considered as the period of Third Generation of computers.
- The third generation computers were developed by using the Integrated Circuit (IC) technology.
- In comparison to the computers of the second generation, the size of the computers of the third generation was smaller.
- In comparison to the computers of the second generation, the computing time taken by the computers of the third generation was lesser.
- The third generation computer consumed less power and also generated less heat.
- The maintenance cost of the computers in the third generation was also low.
- The computer system of the computers of the third generation was easier for commercial use.

Third Generation

Fig 1.23: Third Generation Computer

1.24 Fourth Generation

- The period 1972 to 2010 is roughly considered as the fourth generation of computers.
- The fourth generation computers were developed by using microprocessor technology.
- By coming to fourth generation, computer became very small in size, it became portable.
- The machine of fourth generation started generating very low amount of heat.
- It is much faster and accuracy became more reliable.
- The production cost reduced to very low in comparison to the previous generation.
- It became available for the common people as well.

Fig 1.24: Fourth Generation Computer

1.25 Fifth Generation

- The period 2010 to till date and beyond, roughly considered as the period of fifth generation of computers.
- By the time, the computer generation was being categorized on the basis of hardware only, but the fifth generation technology also included software.
- The computers of the fifth generation had high capability and large memory capacity.
- Working with computers of this generation was fast and multiple tasks could be performed simultaneously.
- Some of the popular advanced technologies of the fifth generation include Artificial intelligence, Quantum computation, Nanotechnology, Parallel processing, etc.

Fig 1.25: Fifth Generation Computer

1.3 Computer Types:

1.31 Computer sizes and power

Computers can be generally classified by size and power as follows, though there is considerable overlap:

- Personal computer: A small, single-user computer based on a microprocessor.
- Workstation: A powerful, single-user computer. A workstation is like a personal computer, but it has a more powerful microprocessor and, in general, a higher-quality monitor.
- Minicomputer: A multi-user computer capable of supporting up to hundreds of users simultaneously.
- Mainframe: A powerful multi-user computer capable of supporting many hundreds or thousands of users simultaneously.
- Supercomputer: An extremely fast computer that can perform hundreds of millions of instructions per second.

1.32 Supercomputer and Mainframe

Supercomputer is a broad term for one of the fastest computers currently available. Supercomputers are very expensive and are employed for specialized applications that require immense amounts of mathematical calculations (number crunching). For example, weather forecasting requires a supercomputer. Other uses of supercomputers include scientific simulations, (animated) graphics, fluid dynamic calculations, nuclear energy research, electronic design, and analysis of geological data (e.g. in petrochemical prospecting). Perhaps the best known supercomputer manufacturer is Cray Research.

Mainframe was a term originally referring to the cabinet containing the central processor unit or "main frame" of a room-filling Stone Age batch machine. After the emergence of smaller "minicomputer" designs in the early 1970s, the traditional big iron machines were described as "mainframe computers" and eventually just as mainframes. Nowadays a Mainframe is a very large and expensive computer capable of supporting hundreds, or even thousands, of users simultaneously. The chief difference between a supercomputer and a mainframe is that a supercomputer channels all its power into executing a few programs as fast as possible, whereas a mainframe uses its power to execute many programs concurrently. In some ways, mainframes are more powerful than supercomputers because they support more simultaneous programs. But supercomputers can execute a single program faster than a mainframe. The distinction between small mainframes and minicomputers is vague, depending really on how the manufacturer wants to market its machines.

1.33 Minicomputer

It is a midsize computer. In the past decade, the distinction between large minicomputers and small mainframes has blurred, however, as has the distinction between small minicomputers and workstations. But in general, a minicomputer is a multiprocessing system capable of supporting from up to 200 users simultaneously.

1.34 Workstation

It is a type of computer used for engineering applications (CAD/CAM), desktop publishing, software development, and other types of applications that require a moderate amount of computing power and relatively high quality graphics capabilities. Workstations generally come with a large, high-resolution graphics screen, at large amount of RAM, built-in network support, and a graphical user interface. Most workstations also have a mass storage device such as a disk drive, but a special type of workstation, called a diskless workstation, comes without a disk drive. The most common operating systems for workstations are UNIX and Windows NT. Like personal computers, most workstations are single-user computers. However, workstations are typically linked together to form a local-area network, although they can also be used as stand-alone systems.

N.B.: In networking, workstation refers to any computer connected to a local-area network. It could be a workstation or a personal computer.

1.35 Personal computer:

It can be defined as a small, relatively inexpensive computer designed for an individual user. In price, personal computers range anywhere from a few hundred pounds to over five thousand pounds. All are based on the microprocessor technology that enables manufacturers to put an entire CPU on one chip. Businesses use personal computers for word processing, accounting, desktop publishing, and for running spreadsheet and database management applications. At home, the most popular use for personal computers is for playing games and recently for surfing the Internet.

Personal computers first appeared in the late 1970s. One of the first and most popular personal computers was the Apple II, introduced in 1977 by Apple Computer. During the late 1970s and early 1980s, new models and competing operating systems seemed to appear daily. Then, in 1981, IBM entered the fray with its first personal computer, known as the IBM PC. The IBM PC quickly became the personal computer of choice, and most other personal computer manufacturers fell by the wayside. P.C. is short for personal computer or IBM PC. One of the few companies to survive IBM's onslaught was Apple Computer, which remains a major player in the personal computer marketplace. Other companies adjusted to IBM's dominance by building IBM clones, computers that were internally almost the same as the IBM PC, but that cost less.

Because IBM clones used the same microprocessors as IBM PCs, they were capable of running the same software. Over the years, IBM has lost much of its influence in directing the evolution of PCs. Therefore after the release of the first PC by IBM the term PC increasingly came to mean IBM or IBM-compatible personal computers, to the exclusion of other types of personal computers, such as Macintoshes. In recent years, the term PC has become more and more difficult to pin down. In general, though, it applies to any personal computer based on an Intel microprocessor, or on an Intel-compatible microprocessor. For nearly every other component, including the operating system, there are several options, all of which fall under the rubric of PC

Today, the world of personal computers is basically divided between Apple Macintoshes and PCs. The principal characteristics of personal computers are that they are single-user systems and are based on microprocessors. However, although personal computers are designed as single-user systems, it is common to link them together to form a network. In terms of power, there is great variety. At the high end, the distinction between personal computers and workstations has faded. High-end models of the Macintosh and PC offer the same computing power and graphics capability as low-end workstations by Sun Microsystems, Hewlett-Packard, and DEC.

1.36 Personal Computer Types

Actual personal computers can be generally classified by size and chassis / case. The chassis or case is the metal frame that serves as the structural support for electronic components. Every computer system requires at least one chassis to house the circuit boards and wiring. The chassis also contains slots for expansion boards. If you want to insert more boards than there are slots, you will need an expansion chassis, which provides additional slots. There are two basic flavours of chassis designs–desktop models and tower models–but there are many variations on these two basic types. Then come the portable computers that are computers small enough to carry. Portable computers include notebook and subnotebook computers, hand-held computers, palmtops, and PDAs.

1.37 Tower model

The term refers to a computer in which the power supply, motherboard, and mass storage devices are stacked on top of each other in a cabinet. This is in contrast to desktop models, in which these components are housed in a more compact box. The main advantage of tower models is that there are fewer space constraints, which makes installation of additional storage devices easier.

1.38 Desktop model

A computer designed to fit comfortably on top of a desk, typically with the monitor sitting on top of the computer. Desktop model computers are broad and low, whereas tower model computers are narrow and tall. Because of their shape, desktop model computers are generally limited to three internal mass storage devices. Desktop models designed to be very small are sometimes referred to as slim line models.

1.39 Notebook computer

An extremely lightweight personal computer. Notebook computers typically weigh less than 6 pounds and are small enough to fit easily in a briefcase. Aside from size, the principal difference between a notebook computer and a personal computer is the display screen. Notebook computers use a variety of techniques, known as flat-panel technologies, to produce a lightweight and non-bulky display screen. The quality of notebook display screens varies considerably. In terms of computing power, modern notebook computers are nearly equivalent to personal computers. They have the same CPUs, memory capacity, and disk drives. However, all this power in a small package is expensive. Notebook computers cost about twice as much as equivalent regular-sized computers. Notebook computers come with battery packs that enable you to run them without plugging them in. However, the batteries need to be recharged every few hours.

1.40 Laptop computer

A small, portable computer -- small enough that it can sit on your lap. Nowadays, laptop computers are more frequently called notebook computers.

1.41 Subnotebook computer

A portable computer that is slightly lighter and smaller than a full-sized notebook computer. Typically, subnotebook computers have a smaller keyboard and screen, but are otherwise equivalent to notebook computers.

1.42 Hand-held computer

A portable computer that is small enough to be held in one's hand. Although extremely convenient to carry, handheld computers have not replaced notebook computers because of their small keyboards and screens. The most popular hand-held computers are those that are specifically designed to provide PIM (personal information manager) functions, such as a calendar and address book. Some manufacturers are trying to solve the small keyboard problem by replacing the keyboard with an electronic pen. However, these pen-based devices rely on handwriting recognition technologies, which are still in their infancy. Hand-held computers are also called PDAs, palmtops and pocket computers.

1.43 Palmtop

A small computer that literally fits in your palm. Compared to full-size computers, palmtops are severely limited, but they are practical for certain functions such as phone books and calendars. Palmtops that use a pen rather than a keyboard for input are often called hand-held computers or PDAs. Because of their small size, most palmtop computers do not include disk drives. However, many contain PCMCIA slots in which you can insert disk drives, modems, memory, and other devices. Palmtops are also called PDAs, hand-held computers and pocket computers.

1.44 PDA

Short for personal digital assistant, a handheld device that combines computing, telephone/fax, and networking features. A typical PDA can function as a cellular phone, fax sender, and personal organizer. Unlike portable computers, most PDAs are pen-based, using a stylus rather than a keyboard for input. This means that they also incorporate handwriting recognition features. Some PDAs can also react to voice input by using voice recognition technologies. The field of PDA was pioneered by Apple Computer, which introduced the Newton MessagePad in 1993. Shortly thereafter, several other manufacturers offered similar products. To date, PDAs have had only modest success in the marketplace, due to their high price tags and limited applications. However, many experts believe that PDAs will eventually become common gadgets.

PDAs are also called palmtops, hand-held computers and pocket computers.

1.5 Bits,Bytes & Words:

1.51 Bits – binary digits

Computer memory stores the data in bits. Each bit stores the value either 0 or 1. Inside the Computer, there are electronic switches which stores the bit values; either 0 or 1. If the switch is OFF means, that represents 0 & the switch is ON means that represents 1. That means, Computer can understand the data in "0"s and "1"s. We normally use bits to represent processor architecture or design; 32-bit processor, 64-bit processor etc. 64-bit processor can do the computations faster than 32-bit processor.

There must be a data transfer between Computer Memory (RAM – Random Access Memory) and the Computer Processor (CPU). The data transfer happen through BUSES. Each BUS carries N-number of bits; depends on the Computer Architecture. Each BUS has wires to transfer the bits; 16-bit BUS carries 16-bits at a time, and it has 16 wires to transfer each bit. BUSES are used to carry the information between one components to another Component in the Computer.

Mostly, we don't directly deal with the Computer bits; there are computer languages that allows to directly deal with the computer bits. "C" language provides some features to allow the programmers to directly deal with the bits.

How do we represents the data other than 0 & 1; example, characters *('A', 'h' etc.).?* The answer is Byte; another term, we use in the computer terminology is Bytes.

1.52 Bytes

Byte is a grouping of consecutive bits. Usually 8-bits represent a Byte. Generally we use Byte(s) to represents characters; each byte can store the values from 0-255. That means, we can store one of the character from 0-255; in 1 Byte.

The most common term we use in Computers terminology is Bytes. Computer Programs read & write the Bytes from the Memory; also read and write the Bytes to the File Storage; and for the data processing use Bytes; file sizes will display in Bytes and etc.,.

How internally Bytes store that data? Simple, it is Bits. The Byte representation of a character '**A**'
is:

ASCII Character value of 'A' is 65. Bit representation *(binary representation)* of 'A' in a Byte is below:

0
1
0
0
0
0
0
1

Note that, it is not compulsory that 8-bits are used for a Byte in all the Systems. Number of bits used for a Byte is depends on the System Architecture. Commonly we use 8-bits for a Byte.

1.53 WORDs

WORDs are also consecutive bits or bytes. This term mostly we use for CPU registers. Generally, each WORD has length 16-bits. CPU Registers are used to store small piece of information while doing the calculations or processing the data. These are helpful to improve the performance of the System while doing the calculation or processing.

1.6 CPU(central processing unit):

The **CPU** is the brain of a computer, containing all the circuitry needed to process input, store data, and output results.

The CPU is constantly following instructions of computer programs that tell it which data to process and how to process it. Without a CPU, we could not run programs on a computer.

For example, a simple calculator program might instruct the CPU to take two numbers, 2 and 2, add them, and send back the result.

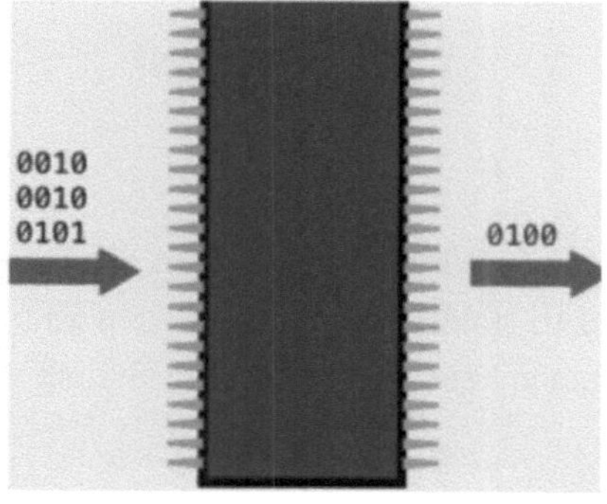

Fig 1.6: CPU

The CPU can process those instructions easily, thanks to a control unit that knows how to interpret program instructions and an Arithmetic Logic Unit (ALU) that knows how to add numbers. With the control unit and ALU combined, the CPU can process much more complex programs than a simple calculator.

1.61 Inside the CPU

At the hardware level, a CPU is an **integrated circuit**, also known as a **chip**. An integrated circuit "integrates" millions or billions of tiny electrical parts, arranging them into circuits and fitting them all into a compact box.

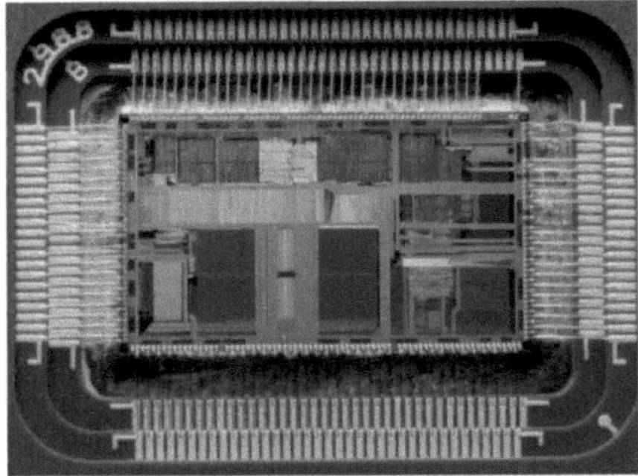

Fig 1.61: CPU Chip

An Intel 80486DX2 CPU chip. *Source:* Wikipedia Commons

1.7 Primary Memory & Secondary Memory:

A memory is just like a human brain. It is used to store data and instructions. Computer memory is the storage space in the computer, where datas to be processed and instructions required for processing are stored. The memory is divided into large number of small parts called cells. Each location or cell has a unique address, which varies from zero to memory size minus one. For example, if the computer has 64k words, then this memory unit has 64 * 1024 = 65536 memory locations. The address of these locations varies from 0 to 65535.

1.71 Memory is primarily of three types –

- Cache Memory
- Primary Memory/Main Memory
- Secondary Memory

1.72 Cache Memory

Cache memory is a very high speed semiconductor memory which can speed up the CPU. It acts as a buffer between the CPU and the main memory. It is used to hold those parts of data and program which are most frequently used by the CPU. The parts of data and programs are transferred from the disk to cache memory by the operating system, from where the CPU can access them.

Fig 1.72: Cache Memory

Advantages
The advantages of cache memory are as follows –

- Cache memory is faster than main memory
- It consumes less access time as compared to main memory.
- It stores the program that can be executed within a short period of time.
- It stores data for temporary use.

Disadvantages

The disadvantages of cache memory are as follows –

- Cache memory has limited capacity.
- It is very expensive.

1.73 Primary Memory (Main Memory)

Primary memory holds only those data and instructions on which the computer is currently working. It has a limited capacity and data is lost when power is switched off. It is generally made up of semiconductor device. These memories are not as fast as registers. The data and instruction required to be processed resides in the main memory. It is divided into two subcategories RAM and ROM.

Fig 1.73: RAM

Characteristics of Main Memory

- These are semiconductor memories.
- It is known as the main memory.
- Usually volatile memory.
- Data is lost in case power is switched off.
- It is the working memory of the computer.
- Faster than secondary memories.
- A computer cannot run without the primary memory.

1.74 Secondary Memory

This type of memory is also known as external memory or non-volatile. It is slower than the main memory. These are used for storing data/information permanently. CPU directly does not access these memories; instead they are accessed via input-output routines. The contents of secondary memories are first transferred to the main memory, and then the CPU can access it. For example, disk, CD-ROM, DVD, etc.

Fig 1.74: Hard disk

Characteristics of Secondary Memory

- These are magnetic and optical memories.
- It is known as the backup memory.
- It is a non-volatile memory.
- Data is permanently stored even if power is switched off.
- It is used for storage of data in a computer.
- Computer may run without the secondary memory.
- Slower than primary memories.

1.8 Ports & connections:

A port is a physical docking point using which an external device can be connected to the computer. It can also be programmatic docking point through which information flows from a program to the computer or over the Internet.

Characteristics of Ports

A port has the following characteristics –

- External devices are connected to a computer using cables and ports.
- Ports are slots on the motherboard into which a cable of external device is plugged in.
- Examples of external devices attached via ports are the mouse, keyboard, monitor, microphone, speakers, etc.

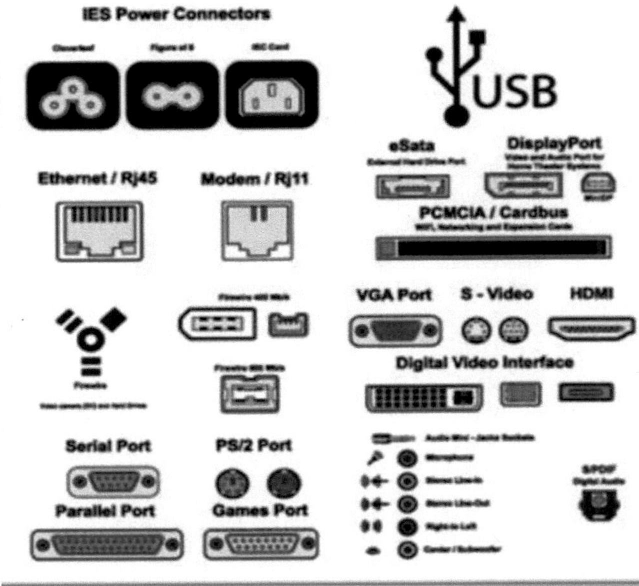

Fig 1.8: Ports

Let us now discuss a few important types of ports –

1.81 Serial Port

- Used for external modems and older computer mouse
- Two versions: 9 pin, 25 pin model
- Data travels at 115 kilobits per second

1.82 Parallel Port

- Used for scanners and printers
- Also called printer port
- 25 pin model
- IEEE 1284-compliant Centronics port

1.83 PS/2 Port

- Used for old computer keyboard and mouse
- Also called mouse port
- Most of the old computers provide two PS/2 port, each for the mouse and keyboard
- IEEE 1284-compliant Centronics port

1.84 Universal Serial Bus (or USB) Port

- It can connect all kinds of external USB devices such as external hard disk, printer, scanner, mouse, keyboard, etc.
- It was introduced in 1997.
- Most of the computers provide two USB ports as minimum.
- Data travels at 12 megabits per seconds.

- USB compliant devices can get power from a USB port.

1.85 (Video Graphics Array)VGA Port

- Connects monitor to a computer's video card.
- It has 15 holes.
- Similar to the serial port connector. However, serial port connector has pins, VGA port has holes.

1.86 Power Connector

- Three-pronged plug.
- Connects to the computer's power cable that plugs into a power bar or wall socket.

1.87 Fire wire Port

- Transfers large amount of data at very fast speed.
- Connects camcorders and video equipment to the computer.
- Data travels at 400 to 800 megabits per seconds.
- Invented by Apple.
- It has three variants: 4-Pin FireWire 400 connector, 6-Pin FireWire 400 connector, and 9-Pin FireWire 800 connector.

1.88 Modem Port

- Connects a PC's modem to the telephone network.

1.89 Ethernet Port

- Connects to a network and high speed Internet.
- Connects the network cable to a computer.

- This port resides on an Ethernet Card.
- Data travels at 10 megabits to 1000 megabits per seconds depending upon the network bandwidth.

1.90 Game Port

- Connect a joystick to a PC
- Now replaced by USB

1.91 Digital Video Interface, DVI port

- Connects Flat panel LCD monitor to the computer's high-end video graphic cards.
- Very popular among video card manufacturers.

1.92 Sockets

- Sockets connect the microphone and speakers to the sound card of the computer.

1.10 Input & Output Devices:

1.101 Peripheral

A peripheral is a "device that is used to put information into or get information out of the computer."

There are three different types of peripherals:

- Input, used to interact with, or send data to the computer (mouse, keyboards, etc.)
- Output, which provides output to the user from the computer (monitors, printers, etc.)

1.102 Input Devices

In computing, an input device is a peripheral (piece of computer hardware equipment) used to provide data and control signals to an information processing system such as a computer or other information appliance. Examples of input devices include keyboards, mice, scanners, digital cameras and joysticks.

Many input devices can be classified according to:

- Modality of input (e.g. mechanical motion, audio, visual, etc.)
- the input is discrete (e.g. key presses) or continuous (e.g. a mouse's position, though digitized into a discrete quantity, is fast enough to be considered continuous)

Pointing devices, which are input devices used to specify a position in space, can further be classified according to:

- Whether the input is direct or indirect. With direct input, the input space coincides with the display space, i.e. pointing is done in the space where visual feedback or the pointer appears. Touchscreens and light pens involve direct input. Examples involving indirect input include the mouse and trackball.
- Whether the positional information is absolute (e.g. on a touch screen) or relative (e.g. with a mouse that can be lifted and repositioned)

Direct input is almost necessarily absolute, but indirect input may be either absolute or relative. For example, digitizing graphics tablets that do not have an embedded screen involve indirect input and sense absolute positions and are often run in an absolute input mode, but they may also be set up to simulate a relative input mode like that of a touchpad, where the stylus or puck can be lifted and repositioned.

Input and output devices make up the hardware interface between a computer and a scanner or 6DOF controller.

1.103 Keyboards

A **keyboard** is a human interface device which is represented as a layout of buttons. Each button, or key, can be used to either input a linguistic character to a computer, or to call upon a particular function of the computer. They act as the main text entry interface for most users. Traditional keyboards use spring-based buttons, though newer variations employ virtual keys, or even projected keyboards. It is typewriter like device composed of a matrix of switches.

Examples of types of keyboards include:

- Keyer
- Keyboard
- Lighted Program Function Keyboard (LPFK)

1.104 Pointing Devices:

Fig 1.104: Mouse

Pointing devices are the most commonly used input devices today. A pointing device is any human interface device that allows a user to input spatial data to a computer. In the case of mice and touchpads, this is usually achieved by detecting movement across a physical surface. Analog devices, such as 3D mice, joysticks, or pointing sticks, function by reporting their angle of deflection. Movements of the pointing device are echoed on the screen by movements of the pointer, creating a simple, intuitive way to navigate a computer's graphical user interface (GUI).

1.105 Composite Devices:

Fig 1.105: Wii Remote with attached strap

Input devices, such as buttons and joysticks, can be combined on a single physical device that could be thought of as a composite device. Many gaming devices have controllers like this. Technically mice are composite devices, as they both track movement and provide buttons for clicking, but composite devices are generally considered to have more than two different forms of input.

- Game controller
- Gamepad (or joy pad)
- Paddle (game controller)
- Jog dial/shuttle (or knob)
- Wii Remote

1.106 Imaging and Input Devices

Fig 1.106: Microsoft Kinect sensor

Video input devices are used to digitize images or video from the outside world into the computer. The information can be stored in a multitude of formats depending on the user's requirement.

- Digital camera
- Digital camcorder
- Portable media player
- Webcam
- Microsoft Kinect Sensor
- Image scanner
- Fingerprint scanner
- Barcode reader
- 3D scanner
- Laser rangefinder
- Eye gaze tracker

1.107 Medical Imaging

- Computed tomography
- Magnetic resonance imaging
- Positron emission tomography
- Medical ultrasonography

1.108 Audio Input Devices

Audio input devices allow a user to send audio info to a computer for processing, recording, or carrying out commands. Devices such as microphones allow users to speak to the computer in order to record a voice message or navigate software.

- Microphones
- MIDI keyboard or other digital musical instrument

1.109 Output Devices

An output device is any piece of computer hardware equipment used to communicate the results of data processing carried out by an information processing system (such as a computer) which converts the electronically generated information into human-readable form.

1.110Display Devices

A display device is an output device that visually conveys text, graphics, and video information. Information shown on a display device is called soft copy because the information exists electronically and is displayed for a temporary period of time. Display devices include CRT monitors, LCD monitors and displays, gas plasma monitors, and televisions.

There are many input and output devices such as multifunction printers and computer-based navigation systems that are used for specialised or unique applications. IN computing, input/output refers to the communication between an information processing system (such as a computer), and the outside world. Inputs are the signals or data received by the system, and outputs are the signals or data sent from it.

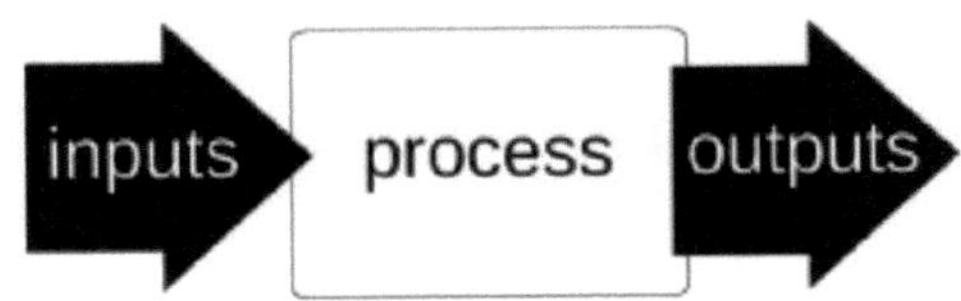

Fig 1.110

Inputs are the signals or data received by the system, and outputs are the signals or data sent from it.

Examples

These examples of output devices also include input/output devices. Printers and visual displays are the most common type of output device for interfacing to people, but voice is becoming increasingly available.

- Speakers
- Headphones
- Screen (Monitor)
- Printer
- Voice output communication aid
- Automotive navigation system
- Braille embosser
- Projector
- Plotter
- Television
- Radio

1.11 Computers in a Network:

Computer Network Types

A computer network is a group of computers linked to each other that enables the computer to communicate with another computer and share their resources, data, and applications.

A computer network can be categorized by their size. A **computer network** is mainly of **four types**:

- LAN(Local Area Network)
- PAN(Personal Area Network)
- MAN(Metropolitan Area Network)
- WAN(Wide Area Network)

1.111 LAN(Local Area Network)

- Local Area Network is a group of computers connected to each other in a small area such as building, office.
- LAN is used for connecting two or more personal computers through a communication medium such as twisted pair, coaxial cable, etc.

- It is less costly as it is built with inexpensive hardware such as hubs, network adapters, and Ethernet cables.
- The data is transferred at an extremely faster rate in Local Area Network.
- Local Area Network provides higher security.

Fig 1.111: LAN

1.112 PAN(Personal Area Network)

- Personal Area Network is a network arranged within an individual person, typically within a range of 10 meters.
- Personal Area Network is used for connecting the computer devices of personal use is known as Personal Area Network.
- **Thomas Zimmerman** was the first research scientist to bring the idea of the Personal Area Network.
- Personal Area Network covers an area of **30 feet.**
- Personal computer devices that are used to develop the personal area network are the laptop, mobile phones, media player and play stations.

Fig 1.112: PAN

1.113 MAN(Metropolitan Area Network)

A metropolitan area network is a network that covers a larger geographic area by interconnecting a different LAN to form a larger network.

- Government agencies use MAN to connect to the citizens and private industries.
- In MAN, various LANs are connected to each other through a telephone exchange line.
- The most widely used protocols in MAN are RS-232, Frame Relay, ATM, ISDN, OC-3, ADSL, etc.
- It has a higher range than Local Area Network(LAN).

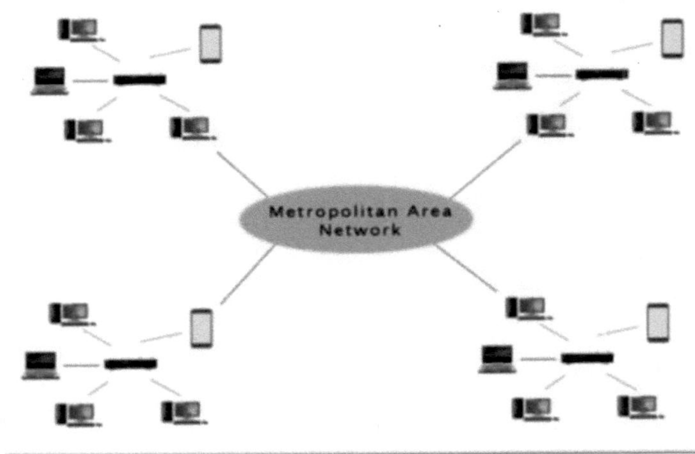

Fig 1.113: MAN

Uses of Metropolitan Area Network:

- MAN is used in communication between the banks in a city.
- It can be used in an Airline Reservation.
- It can be used in a college within a city.
- It can also be used for communication in the military.

1.114 WAN(Wide Area Network)

- A Wide Area Network is a network that extends over a large geographical area such as states or countries.
- A Wide Area Network is quite bigger network than the LAN.
- A Wide Area Network is not limited to a single location, but it spans over a large geographical area through a telephone line, fibre optic cable or satellite links.
- The internet is one of the biggest WAN in the world.
- A Wide Area Network is widely used in the field of Business, government, and education.

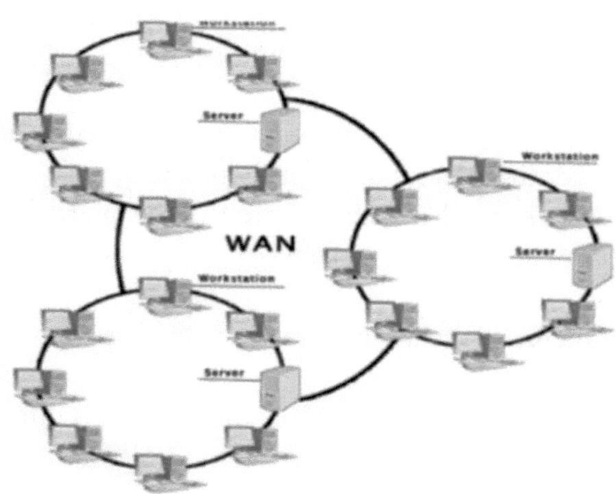

Fig 1.114: WAN

Examples of Wide Area Network:

- **Mobile Broadband:** A 4G network is widely used across a region or country.
- **Last mile:** A telecom company is used to provide the internet services to the customers in hundreds of cities by connecting their home with fiber.
- **Private network:** A bank provides a private network that connects the 44 offices. This network is made by using the telephone leased line provided by the telecom company.

Advantages of Wide Area Network:

Following are the advantages of the Wide Area Network:

- **Geographical area:** A Wide Area Network provides a large geographical area. Suppose if the branch of our office is in a different city then we can connect with them through WAN. The internet provides a leased line through which we can connect with another branch.
- **Centralized data:** In case of WAN network, data is centralized. Therefore, we do not need to buy the emails, files or back up servers.
- **Get updated files:** Software companies work on the live server. Therefore, the programmers get the updated files within seconds.
- **Exchange messages:** In a WAN network, messages are transmitted fast. The web application like Facebook, WhatsApp, Skype allows you to communicate with friends.
- **Sharing of software and resources:** In WAN network, we can share the software and other resources like a hard drive and RAM.
- **Global business:** We can do the business over the internet globally.
- **High bandwidth:** If we use the leased lines for our company then this gives the high bandwidth. The high bandwidth increases the data transfer rate which in turn increases the productivity of our company.

Disadvantages of Wide Area Network:

The following are the disadvantages of the Wide Area Network:

- **Security issue:** A WAN network has more security issues as compared to LAN and MAN network as all the technologies are combined together that creates the security problem.
- **Needs Firewall & Antivirus software:** The data is transferred on the internet which can be changed or hacked by the hackers, so the firewall needs to be used. Some people can inject the virus in our system so antivirus is needed to protect from such a virus.
- **High Setup cost:** An installation cost of the WAN network is high as it involves the purchasing of routers and switches.
- **Troubleshooting problems:** It covers a large area so fixing the problem is difficult.

1.115 Network Hardware:

Computer Network Components:

Computer network components are the *major parts* which are needed to *install the software*. Some important network components are **NIC**, **switch**, **cable**, **hub**, **router**, and **modem**. Depending on the type of network that we need to install, some network components can also be removed. For example, the wireless network does not require a cable.

Following are the major components required to install a network:

1.116 NIC

- NIC stands for network interface card.
- NIC is a hardware component used to connect a computer with another computer onto a network
- It can support a transfer rate of 10,100 to 1000 Mb/s.
- The MAC address or physical address is encoded on the network card chip which is assigned by the IEEE to identify a network card uniquely. The MAC address is stored in the PROM (Programmable read-only memory).

There are two types of NIC:

- Wired NIC
- Wireless NIC

Wired NIC: The Wired NIC is present inside the motherboard. Cables and connectors are used with wired NIC to transfer data.

Wireless NIC: The wireless NIC contains the antenna to obtain the connection over the wireless network. For example, laptop computer contains the wireless NIC.

1.117 Hub

A Hub is a hardware device that divides the network connection among multiple devices. When computer requests for some information from a network, it first sends the request to the Hub through cable. Hub will broadcast this request to the entire network. All the devices will check whether the request belongs to them or not. If not, the request will be dropped.

The process used by the Hub consumes more bandwidth and limits the amount of communication. Nowadays, the use of hub is obsolete, and it is replaced by more advanced computer network components such as Switches, Routers.

1.118 Switch

A switch is a hardware device that connects multiple devices on a computer network. A Switch contains more advanced features than Hub. The Switch contains the updated table that decides where the data is transmitted or not. Switch delivers the message to the correct destination based on the physical address present in the incoming message. A Switch does not broadcast the message to the entire network like the Hub. It determines the device to whom the message is to be transmitted. Therefore, we can say that switch provides a direct connection between the source and destination. It increases the speed of the network.

1.119 Router

- A router is a hardware device which is used to connect a LAN with an internet connection. It is used to receive, analyse and forward the incoming packets to another network.
- A router works in a **Layer 3 (Network layer)** of the OSI Reference model.
- A router forwards the packet based on the information available in the routing table.
- It determines the best path from the available paths for the transmission of the packet.

Advantages of Router:

- **Security:** The information which is transmitted to the network will traverse the entire cable, but the only specified device which has been addressed can read the data.
- **Reliability:** If the server has stopped functioning, the network goes down, but no other networks are affected that are served by the router.
- **Performance:** Router enhances the overall performance of the network. Suppose there are 24 workstations in a network generates a same amount of traffic. This increases the traffic load on the network. Router splits the single network into two networks of 12 workstations each, reduces the traffic load by half.

1.120Modem

- A modem is a hardware device that allows the computer to connect to the internet over the existing telephone line.
- A modem is not integrated with the motherboard rather than it is installed on the PCI slot found on the motherboard.
- It stands for Modulator/Demodulator. It converts the digital data into an analog signal over the telephone lines.

Based on the differences in speed and transmission rate, a modem can be classified in the following categories:

- Standard PC modem or Dial-up modem
- Cellular Modem
- Cable modem

1.121 Cables and Connectors

Cable is a transmission media used for transmitting a signal.

There are three types of cables used in transmission:

- Twisted pair cable
- Coaxial cable
- Fibre-optic cable

1.13 Software Basics & Software types:

As you know, the hardware devices need user instructions to function. A set of instructions that achieve a single outcome are called program or procedure. Many programs functioning together to do a task make a software.

For example, a word-processing software enables the user to create, edit and save documents. A web browser enables the user to view and share web pages and multimedia files. There are three categories of software –

- System Software
- Application Software
- Utility Software

1.131 System Software

Software required to run the hardware parts of the computer and other application software are called system software. System software acts as interface between hardware and user applications. An interface is needed because hardware devices or machines and humans speak in different languages.

Machines understand only binary language i.e. 0 (absence of electric signal) and 1 (presence of electric signal) while humans speak in English, French, German, Tamil, Hindi and many other languages. English is the pre-dominant language of interacting with computers. Software is required to convert all human instructions into machine understandable instructions. And this is exactly what system software does.

Based on its function, system software is of three types –

- Operating System
- Language Processor
- Device Drivers

Operating System

System software that is responsible for functioning of all hardware parts and their interoperability to carry out tasks successfully is called operating system (OS). OS is the first software to be loaded into computer memory when the computer is switched on and this is called booting. OS manages a computer's basic functions like storing data in memory, retrieving files from storage devices, scheduling tasks based on priority, etc.

Language Processor

As discussed earlier, an important function of system software is to convert all user instructions into machine understandable language. When we talk of human machine interactions, languages are of three types –

- Machine-level language– This language is nothing but a string of 0s and 1s that the machines can understand. It is completely machine dependent.
- Assembly-level language– This language introduces a layer of abstraction by defining mnemonics. Mnemonics are English like words or symbols used to denote a long string of 0s and 1s. For example, the word "READ" can be defined to mean that computer has to retrieve data from the memory. The complete instruction will also tell the memory address. Assembly level language is machine dependent.
- High level language – This language uses English like statements and is completely independent of machines. Programs written using high level languages are easy to create, read and understand.

Program written in high level programming languages like Java, C++, etc. is called source code. Set of instructions in machine readable form is called object code or machine code. System software that converts source code to object code is called language processor. There are three types of language interpreters–

- Assembler – Converts assembly level program into machine level program.
- Interpreter– Converts high level programs into machine level program line by line.
- Compiler– Converts high level programs into machine level programs at one go rather than line by line.

Device Drivers

System software that controls and monitors functioning of a specific device on computer is called device driver. Each device like printer, scanner, microphone, speaker, etc. that needs to be attached externally to the system has a specific driver associated with it. When you attach a new device, you need to install its driver so that the OS knows how it needs to be managed.

1.132 Application Software

Software that performs a single task and nothing else is called application software. Application softwareis very specialized in their function and approach to solving a problem. So spreadsheet software can only do operations with numbers and nothing else. Hospital management software will manage hospital activities and nothing else. Here are some commonly used application software –

- Word processing
- Spreadsheet
- Presentation
- Database management
- Multimedia tools

1.133Utility Software

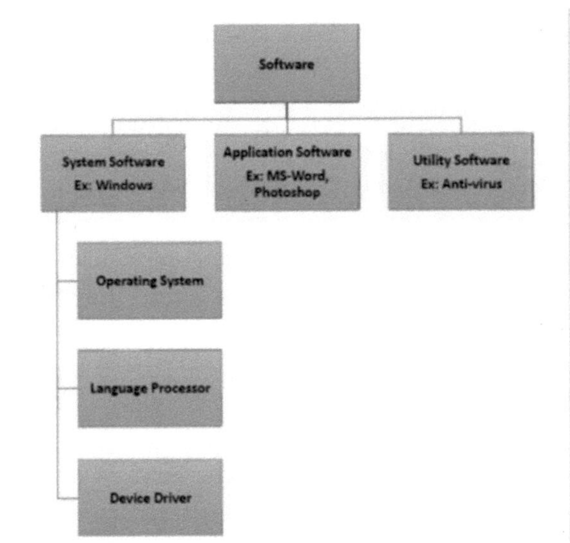

Fig 1.133 Utility Software

Application software that assist system software in doing their work is called utility software. Thus utility software is actually a cross between system software and application software. Examples of utility software include –

- Antivirus software
- File management tools
- Compression tools
- Backup tools
- Disk management tools

1.14 Basics of C program:

Program:

Definition: A program is set of statements or instructions written for a specific task.

Example: Program to find Sum of two numbers. Finding sum of two numbers is the task for which program is supposed to be designed or written.

Every C program will consists of two parts:

1. Syntax
2. Semantics

Syntax: It defines rules & regulations for writing the program. Furthermore it also discuss flow of the program.

Semantics: It defines logic of the program. For example if a program is supposed to written for adding two numbers then the program should & must be designed for adding two numbers only.

1. **Basic Structure of C Program**

A C program involves the following sections:

- Documentations (Documentation Section) - Consists of comments, some description of the program, programmer name and any other useful points that can be referenced later.
- Pre-processorStatements (Link Section) or header files- Provides instruction to the compiler to link function from the library function.
- Global Declarations (Definition Section) - Consists of function declaration and global variables.
- The main() function- Every C program must have a main() function which is the starting point of the program execution.
- Real time example: It is just like main entrance of the college only through which people can take entry.Incase gate is closed then people may not enter.
    - Local Declarations- Variables which are defined & scope is within the main function.
    - Program Statements & Expressions- symbols like (; , :), input & output statements used as a part of syntax.
- User Defined Functions- functions defined by the user (customised definition of the function).

Sample program:

1. **C program to Display "Hello World" message:**

```
/*
Program to display "hello world" message // Documentation section
*/
#include<stdio.h> //header file-consist of all the relevant in-built functions
Void main() // main() function- compilation starts from main()
{ // opening curly bracket to mark beginning of definition of the main() function
printf("Hello World"); //Printf- output function used for displaying user's messages.
}// closing curly bracket to mark end of definition of main() function
```

Executing a C Program:

1. In Linux or Ubuntu operating system:

Step 1: Write a simple C program

After installing the essential packages, let us write a simple C program.

Open Ubuntu's graphical Text Editor and write or copy the following sample program into it:

```
#include<stdio.h>
int main()
```

```
{
printf("\nA sample C program\n\n");
return 0;
}
```

Then save the file with .c extension. In this example, I am naming my C program as sampleProgram.c

Note: Only if the program name is saved with .c extension, color of statements within the program will appear as shown in below sample program 1.1.

Sample program 1.1: sampleprogram.c

Open sampleProgram.c ~/ Save

```
#include<stdio.h>
int main()
{
printf("\nA sample C program\n\n");
return 0;
}
```

Alternatively, you can write the C program through the Terminal in gedit as follows:

```
$ gedit sampleProgram.c
```

This will create a .c file where you can write and save a program.

Step 2: Compile the C program with gcc Compiler

In your Terminal, enter the following command in order to make an executable version of the program you have written

Syntax:

```
$ gcc [programName].c
```

Example:

```
$ gcc sampleProgram.c
```

Make sure your program is located in your Home folder. Otherwise, you will need to specify appropriate paths in this command.

Step 3: Run the program

The final step is to run the compiled C program. Use the following syntax to do so:

```
$ ./a.out
```

2. In Window operating system using turbo C++:

Step 1: Locate the TC.exe file and open it. You will find it at location **C:\TC\BIN**.

Step 2: File > New (as shown in above picture) and then write your C program

```
#include<stdio.h>
int main()
{
printf("hello World!");
return0;
}
```

Step 3: Save the program using F2 (OR file > Save), remember the extension should be ".c". In the below screenshot I have given the name as helloworld.c.

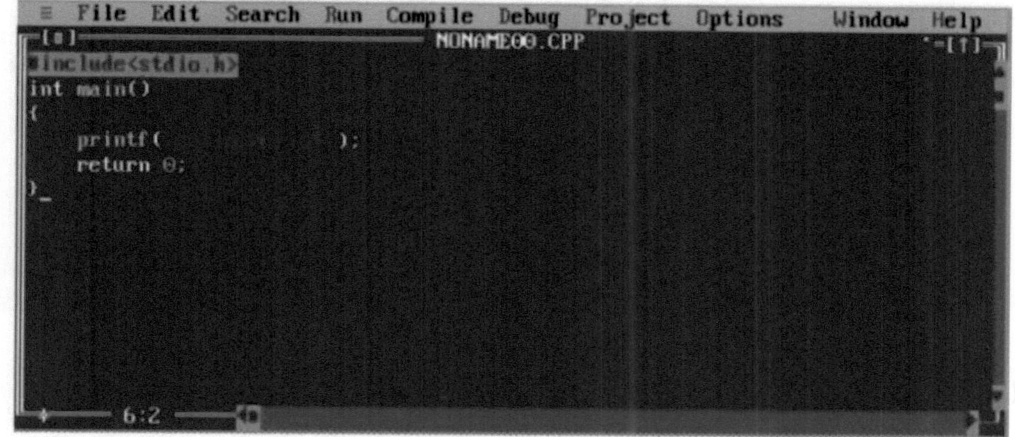

Step 3: Save the program using F2 (OR file > Save), remember the extension should

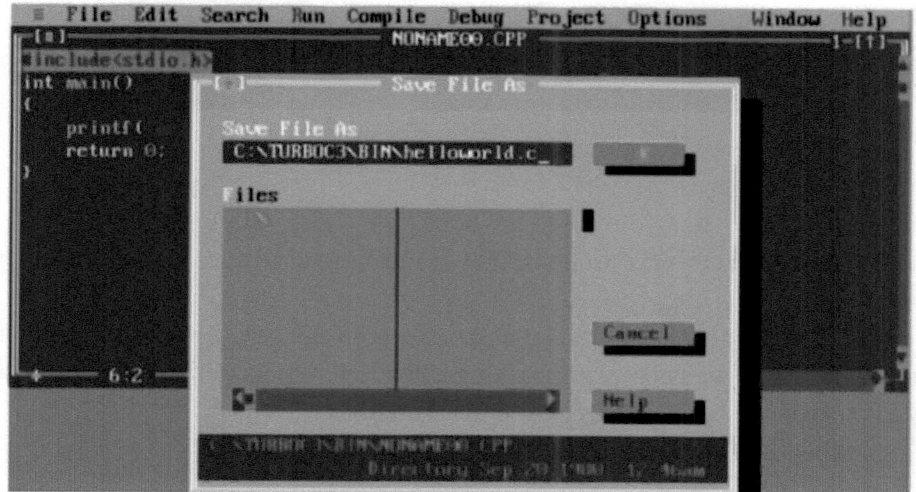

Step 4: Compile the program using Alt + F9 **OR** Compile > Compile (as shown in the below screenshot).

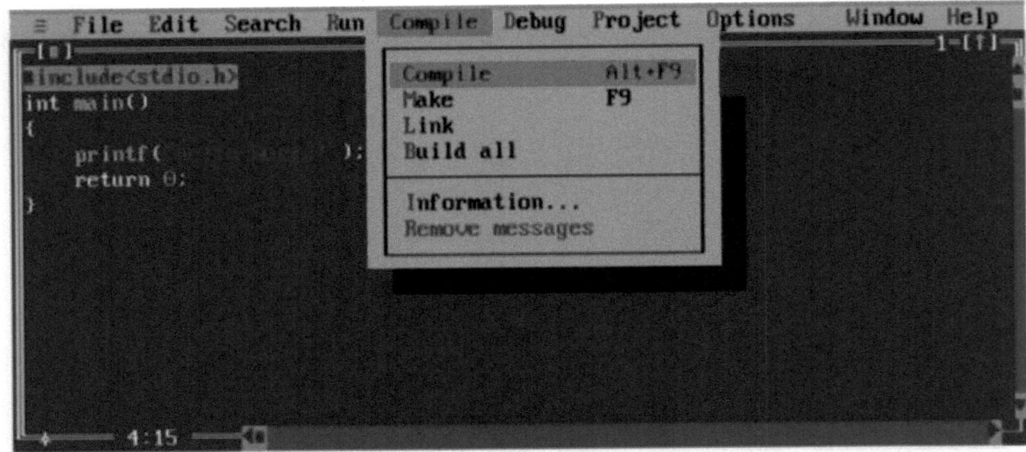

Step 5: Press Ctrl + F9 to Run (or select Run > Run in menu bar) the C program.

Step 6: Alt+F5 to view the output of the program at the output screen.

3. C Tokens:

A token is the smallest element of a program that is meaningful to the compiler.Every word in C program is considered as a token.

Real time example: Tokens are similar to alphabets or words along with Grammar used in English language. In order to learn English language we begin with learning alphabets subsequently framing words & finally meaningful statements. Similarly tokens are basic units required in C language.

Tokens can be classified as follows:

1. Keywords
2. Identifiers
3. Constants
4. Strings
5. Special Symbols
6. Operators

1. **Keywords:**Keywords are pre-defined or reserved words in a programming language. Each keyword is meant to perform a specific function in a program. Since keywords are referred names for a compiler, they can't be used as variable names because by doing so, we are trying to assign a new meaning to the keyword which is not allowed. You cannot redefine keywords. However, you can specify the text to be substituted for keywords before compilation by using C pre-processor directives.Clanguage supports **32** keywords which are given below:

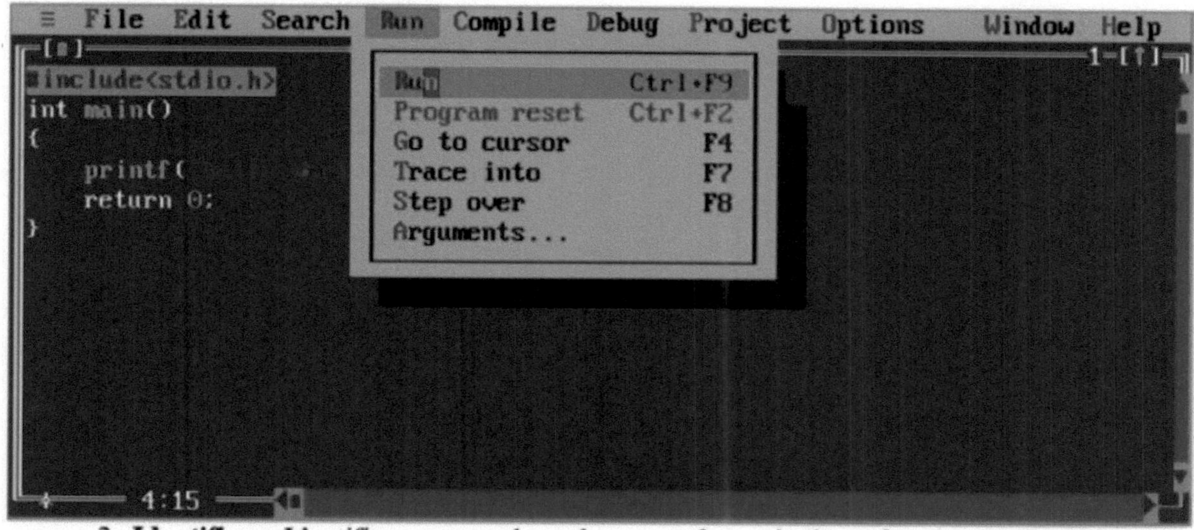

2. Identifiers: Identifiers are used as the general terminology for the naming of variables, functions and arrays. These are user-defined names consisting of an arbitrarily long sequence of letters and digits with either a letter or the underscore (_)as a first character. Identifier names must differ in spelling and case from any keywords. You cannot use keywords as identifiers; they are reserved for special use. Once declared, you can use the identifier in later program statements to refer to the associated value. A special kind of identifier, called a statement label, can be used in go to statement.

There are certain rules that should be followed while naming c identifiers:

- They must begin with a letter or underscore (_).
- They must consist of only letters, digits, or underscore. No other special character is allowed.
- It should not be a keyword.
- It must not contain white spaces(blank space).
- It should be up to 31 characters long as only the first 31 characters are significant.
- **Main:** method name.
- **A:** variable name.

3. Constants: Constants are also like normal variables. But, the only difference is, their values cannot be modified by the program once they are defined. Constants refer to fixed values. They are also called literals.
Constants may belong to any of the data type

auto double int struct
break else long switch
case enum register typedef
char extern return union
const float short unsigned
continue for signed void
default goto sizeof volatile
do if static while
Integer constants – Example: 0, 1, 1218, 12482

1. Real or Floating-point constants – Example: 0.0, 1203.03, 30486.184

2. Octal & Hexadecimal constants – Example: octal: (013)8 = (11)10, Hexadecimal: (013)16 = (19)10
3. Character constants -Example: 'a', 'A', 'z'
4. String constants -Example: "Greetings"

4. Strings: Strings are nothing but an array (group) of characters ended with a null character ('\0'). This null character indicates the end of the string. Strings are always enclosed in double-quotes, Whereas, a character is enclosed in single quotes in C.**Declarations for String:**

- char string[20] = {'g', 'r', 'e', 'e', 't', 'i', 'n', 'g', '\0'};
- char string[20] = "greetings";
- char string [] = "greetings";
- When we declare char as "string[20]", 20 bytes of memory space is allocated for holding the string value.
- When we declare char as "string[]", memory space will be allocated as per the requirement during the execution of the program.

5. Special Symbols: The following special symbols are used in C having some special meaning and thus, cannot be used for some other purpose. [] () {}, ; * = #

- **Brackets[]:** Opening and closing brackets are used as array element reference. These indicate single and multidimensional subscripts.
- **Parentheses():** These special symbols are used to indicate function calls and function parameters.
- **Braces{}:** These opening and ending curly braces mark the start and end of a block of code containing more than one executable statement.
- **Comma (,):** It is used to separate more than one statements like for separating parameters in function calls.
- **Colon (:):** It is an operator that essentially invokes something called an initialization list.
- **Semicolon (;):** It is known as a statement terminator. It indicates the end of one logical entity. That's why each individual statement must be ended with a semicolon.
- **Asterisk (*):** It is used to create a pointer variable.
- **Assignment operator (=):** It is used to assign values.
- **Pre-processor (#):** The pre-processor is a macro processor that is used automatically by the compiler to transform your program before actual compilation.

1. **Operators:** Operators are symbols that trigger an action when applied to C variables and other objects. The data items on which operators act upon are called operands.
   Depending on the number of operands that an operator can act upon, operators can be classified as follows:

- **Unary Operators:** Those operators that require only a single operand to act upon are known as unary operators. For Example increment and decrement operators.(decrement operator : 4-- is same as 4-1 , increment operator: 4++ is same as 4+1)
- **Binary Operators:** Those operators that require two operands to act upon are called binary operators. **Binary operators are classified into :**

  1. Arithmetic operators(4+5)

  Example: +,-,*, /, %(modulus)

  2. Relational Operators(5>4)

Example: ==, >=, <=, >, <

3. Logical Operators(0010 || 1100)

Example: AND, OR

4. Assignment Operators(a=4)

Example: =, +=,-+, *=, /=
a+=b can be represented as a= a+b, same case for other assignment operators

5. Conditional Operators(a ? b : c)
6. Bitwise Operators(right shift operator& left shift operator)

CHAPTER TWO

Module-2 READING,PROCESSING ANDWRITING(PRINTING)DATA

As we all know the three essential functions of a computer are **reading, processing** and **writing (printing)** data. Majority of the programs take data as input, and then after processing the processed data is being displayed which is called information. In C programming you can use **scanf()** and **printf()** predefined function to read and print or display data.

Example:

```
#include<stdio.h>
void main()
{
int a,b,c;
printf("Please enter any two numbers: \n");
scanf("%d %d", &a, &b);
c = a + b;
printf("The addition of two number is: %d", c);
}
```

Output:

```
Please enter any two numbers:
12
3
The addition of two number is:15
```

The above program scanf() is used to take input from the user, and respectively printf() is used to display output result on the screen.

I/O operations are useful for a program to interact with users.stdlib is the standard C library for input-output operations. While dealing with input-output operations in C, two important streams play their role.

These are:

1. Standard Input (stdin)
2. Standard Output (stdout)

Standard input or stdin is used for taking input from devices such as the keyboard as a data stream. Standard output or stdout is used for giving output to a device such as a monitor. For using I/O functionality, programmers must include **stdio.h**within the program.

2.1 Reading Characters in C:

The easiest and simplest of all I/O operations are taking a character as input by reading that character from standard input (keyboard).getchar() function can be used to read a single character. This function is alternate to scanf() function.

Syntax:

```
var_name = getchar();
Example:
#include<stdio.h>
void main()
{
char title;
title = getchar(); /*for example if value of title is 'a', then getchar() fucntion will help in reading
*/the assigned value
}
```

In above example character assigned to 'title' variable can be read using getchar() function.

2.2 Writing Character in C:

Similar to getchar() there is another function putchar() which is used to write characters, but one at a time.

Syntax:

```
putchar(var_name);
```

Example:

```
#include<stdio.h>
void main()
{
char result ='P';
putchar(result);
putchar('\n');
}
```

2.3 Formatted Input:

It refers to an input data which has been arranged in a specific format. This is possible in C using scanf(). The scanf() function reads formatted input from the standard input such as keyboards.

Syntax:

```
scanf("format specifier", &variable list);
```

Example:

```
#include <stdio.h>
int main()
{
int testInteger;
printf("Enter an integer: ");
scanf("%d", &testInteger);
printf("Number = %d",testInteger);
return 0;
}
```

Output:

Enter an Integer: 5

Number=4

In above example, we have used %d format specifier inside the scanf() function to take int input from the user. When the user enters an integer, it is stored in the testInteger variable. Notice, that we have used &testInteger inside scanf(). It is because &testInteger gets the address of testInteger, and the value entered by the user is stored in that address.

For float variables %f format specifire is used within scanf() function, for character variables %c is being used.

2.4 Formatted output:

In C programming, printf() is one of the main output function. The function sends formatted output to the screen. For example,

1. Sample program to print C Programming

```
#include <stdio.h>
int main()
{
// Displays the string inside quotations
printf("C Programming");
return 0;
}
```

Output:

C Programming

How does this program work?

- All valid C programs must contain the main() function. The code execution begins from the start of the main()function.
- The printf() is a library function to send formatted output to the screen. The function prints the string inside quotations.
- To use printf() in our program, we need to include stdio.h header file using the #include<stdio.h>statement.
- The return 0; statement inside the main() function is the "Exit status" of the program. **It's optional.**

Example 2: Integer Output

```
#include <stdio.h>
int main()
{
int testInteger = 5;
printf("Number = %d", testInteger);
return 0;
}
```

Output

Number = 5

We use %d format specifier to print int types. Here, the %d inside the quotations will be replaced by the value of testInteger.

Similarly %f and %c are used as a format specifiers for float and character values inside printf() function respectively.

Example 3: float and double Output

```
#include <stdio.h>
int main()
{
float number1 = 13.5;
double number2 = 12.4;
printf("number1 = %f\n", number1);
printf("number2 = %lf", number2);
return 0;
}
```

Output

number1 = 13.500000

number2 = 12.400000

What is a Conditional Statement in C?

2.5 Conditional Statements in C programming are used to make decisions based on the conditions. Conditional statements execute sequentially when there is no condition around the statements. If you put some condition for a block of statements, the execution flow may change based on the result evaluated by the condition. This process is called decision making in 'C.'

In 'C' programming conditional statements are possible with the help of the following two constructs:

1. If statement
2. If-else statement

It is also called as branching as a program decides which statement to execute based on the result of the evaluated condition.

What is a Conditional Statement?

- If statement
- Relational Operators
- The If-Else statement
- Conditional Expressions
- Nested If-else Statements
- Nested Else-if statements

2.51 If statement

It is one of the powerful conditional statement. If statement is responsible for modifying the flow of execution of a program. If statement is always used with a condition. The condition is evaluated first before executing any statement inside the body of If. The syntax for if statement is as follows:

```
if (condition)
instruction;
```

Following program illustrates the use of *if*construct in 'C' programming:

```
#include<stdio.h>
int main()
{
int num1=1;
int num2=2;
if(num1<num2) //test-condition
{
printf("num1 is smaller than num2");
}
return 0;
}
```

Output:

num1 is smaller than num2

The above program illustrates the use of *if* construct to check equality of two numbers.

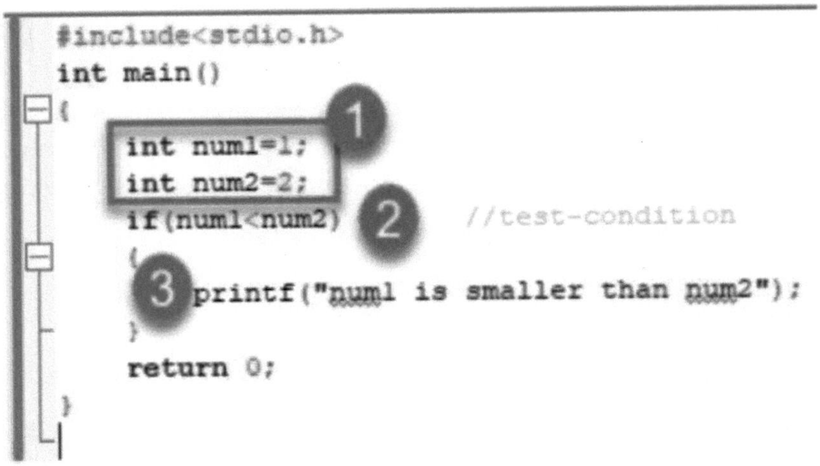

```
#include<stdio.h>
int main()
{
    int num1=1;
    int num2=2;
    if(num1<num2)          //test-condition
    {
        printf("num1 is smaller than num2");
    }
    return 0;
}
```

1. In the above program, we have initialized two variables with num1, num2 with value as 1, 2 respectively.
2. Then, we have used if with a test-expression to check which number is the smallest and which number is the largest. We have used a relational expression in if construct. Since the value of num1 is smaller than num2, the condition will evaluate to true.
3. Thus it will print the statement inside the block of If. After that, the control will go outside of the block and program will be terminated with a successful result.

2.52 Relational Operators

C has six relational operators that can be used to formulate a Boolean expression for making a decision and testing conditions, which returns true or false:

<Less than

<= less than or equal to

>Greater than

>= greater than or equal to

== Equal to

!= not equal to

Notice that the equal test (==) is different from the assignment operator (=) because it is one of the most common problems that a programmer faces by mixing them up.

For example:

```
int x = 41;
x =x+ 1;
if (x == 42) {
printf("You succeed!");}
```

Output:

You succeed

Keep in mind that a condition that evaluates to a non-zero value is considered as true.

For example:

```
int present = 1;
if (present)
printf("There is someone present in the classroom \n");
```

Output:
There is someone present in the classroom

2.53 The If-Else statement

```
int present = 1;
if (present)
printf("There is someone present in the classroom \n");
```

Output:

There is someone present in the classroom

2.53 The If-Else statement

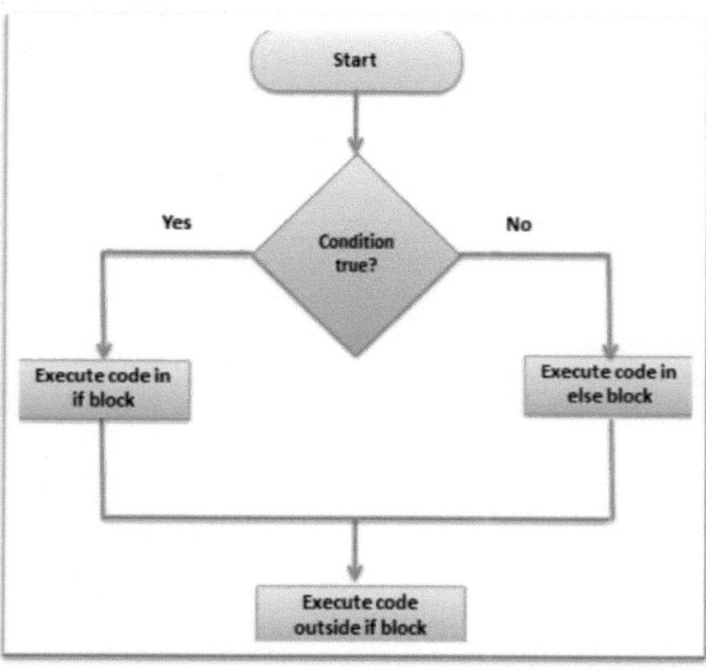

Fig: 2.53

The if-else is statement is an extended version of If. The general form of if-else is as follows:

```
If (test-expression)
{
True block of statements
}
Else
{
False block of statements
}
Statements;
```

In this type of a construct, if the value of test-expression is true, then the true block of statements will be executed (code associated with if). If the value of test-expression if false, then the false block of statements will be executed (code associated with else). In any case, after the execution, the control will be automatically transferred to the statements appearing outside the block of *If*.

Following programs illustrate the use of the if-else construct:

We will initialize a variable with some value and write a program to determine if the value is less than ten or greater than ten.

Let's start.

```
#include<stdio.h>
int main()
{
int num=19;
if(num<10)
{
printf("The value is less than 10");
}
else
{
printf("The value is greater than 10");
}
return 0;
}
```

Output:

The value is greater than 10

```
#include<stdio.h>
int main()
{
    int num=19;
    if(num<10)
    {
        printf("The value is less than 10");
    }
    else
    {
        printf("The value is greater than 10");
    }
    return 0;
}
```

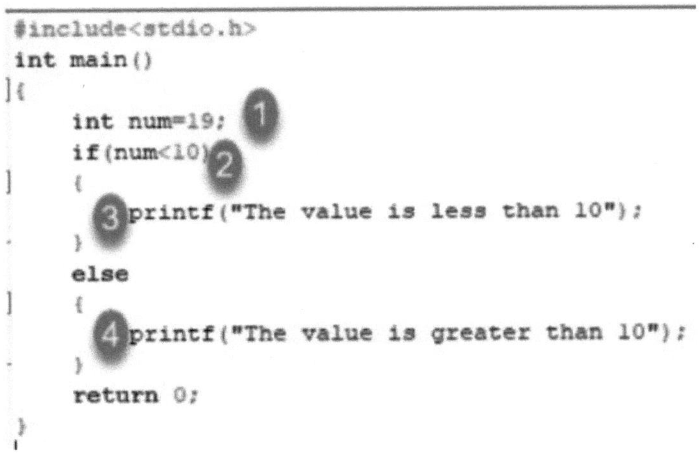

1. We have initialized a variable with value 19. We have to find out whether the number is bigger or smaller than 10 using a 'C' program. To do this, we have used the ***if-else*** construct.
2. Here we have provided a condition num<10 because we have to compare our value with 10.
3. As you can see the first block is always a true block which means, if the value of test-expression is true then the first block which is If, will be executed.
4. The second block is an else block. This block contains the statements which will be executed if the value of the test-expression becomes false. In our program, the value of num is greater than ten hence the test-condition becomes false and else block is executed. Thus, our output will be from an else block which is "The value is greater than 10". After the ***if-else***, the program will terminate with a successful result.

In 'C' programming we can use multiple if-else constructs within each other which are referred to as nesting of if-else statements.

2.54 Conditional Expressions

There is another way to express an if-else statement is by introducing the?: operator. In a conditional expression the ?: operator has only one statement associated with the if and the else.

The conditional operator is kind of similar to the statement as it does follow the same algorithm as of statement but the conditional operator takes less space and helps to write the if-else statements in the shortest way possible.

Syntax:

The conditional operator is of the form

variable = Expression1 ? Expression2 : Expression3

It can be visualized into if-else statement as:

```
if(Expression1)
{
variable = Expression2;
}
else
{
variable = Expression3;
}
```

Since the Conditional Operator '?:' takes three operands to work, hence they are also called **ternary operators .**

Working:

Here, **Expression1**is the condition to be evaluated. If the condition (**Expression1**) is true then **Expression2** will be executed and the result will be returned. Otherwise, if the condition(**Expression1**) is false then **Expression3** will be executed and the result will be returned.

2.55 Nested If-else Statements

When a series of decision is required, nested if-else is used. Nesting means using one if-else statement within another one.

Let's write a program to illustrate the use of nested if-else.

```
#include<stdio.h>
int main()
{
int num=1;
if(num<10)
{
if(num==1)
{
printf("The value is:%d\n",num);
}
else
{
printf("The value is greater than 1");
}
}
else
```

```
{
printf("The value is greater than 10");
}
return 0;
}
```

Output:

The value is:1

The above program checks if a number is less or greater than 10 and prints the result using nested if-else construct.

```
#include<stdio.h>
int main()
{
    int num=19;
    if(num<10)
    {
      printf("The value is less than 10");
    }
    else
    {
      printf("The value is greater than 10");
    }
    return 0;
}
```

1. Firstly, we have declared a variable num with value as 1. Then we have used if-else construct.
2. In the outer if-else, the condition provided checks if a number is less than 10. If the condition is true then and only then it will execute the inner loop. In this case, the condition is true hence the inner block is processed.
3. In the inner block, we again have a condition that checks if our variable contains the value 1 or not. When a condition is true, then it will process the If block otherwise it will process an else block. In this case, the condition is true hence the If a block is executed and the value is printed on the output screen.
4. The above program will print the value of a variable and exit with success.

Try changing the value of variable see how the program behaves.

NOTE: In nested if-else, we have to be careful with the indentation because multiple if-else constructs are involved in this process, so it becomes difficult to figure out individual constructs.

2.56 Nested Else-if statements

Nested else-if is used when multipath decisions are required.

The general syntax of how else-if ladders are constructed in 'C' programming is as follows:

```
if (test - expression 1) {
statement1;
} else if (test - expression 2) {
```

```
Statement2;
} else if (test - expression 3) {
Statement3;
} else if (test - expression n) {
Statement n;
} else {
default;
}
Statement x;
```

This type of structure is known as the else-if ladder. This chain generally looks like a ladder hence it is also called as an else-if ladder. The test-expressions are evaluated from top to bottom. Whenever a true test-expression if found, statement associated with it is executed. When all the n test-expressions becomes false, then the default else statement is executed.

Let us see the actual working with the help of a program.

```
#include<stdio.h>
int main()
{
int marks=83;
if(marks>75){
printf("First class");
}
else if(marks>65){
printf("Second class");
}
else if(marks>55){
printf("Third class");
}
else{
printf("Fourth class");
}
return 0;
}
```

Output:

First class

The above program prints the grade as per the marks scored in a test. We have used the else-if ladder construct in the above program.

```
#include<stdio.h>
int main()
{
    int num=19;        1
    if(num<10)         2
    {
      3 printf("The value is less than 10");
    }
    else
    {
      4 printf("The value is greater than 10");
    }
    return 0;
}
```

1. We have initialized a variable with marks. In the else-if ladder structure, we have provided various conditions.
2. The value from the variable marks will be compared with the first condition since it is true the statement associated with it will be printed on the output screen.
3. If the first test condition turns out false, then it is compared with the second condition.
4. This process will go on until the all expression is evaluated otherwise control will go out of the else-if ladder, and default statement will be printed.

Try modifying the value and notice the change in the output.

Summary

- Decision making or branching statements are used to select one path based on the result of the evaluated expression.
- It is also called as control statements because it controls the flow of execution of a program.
- 'C' provides if and if-else constructs for decision-making statements.
- We can also nest if-else within one another when multiple paths have to be tested.
- The else-if ladder is used when we have to check various ways based upon the result of the expression.

2.6 Looping Statements in C

What is Loop?

Looping Statements in C execute the sequence of statements many times until the stated condition becomes false. A loop in C consists of two parts, a body of a loop and a control statement. The control statement is a combination of some conditions that direct the body of the loop to execute until the specified condition becomes false. The purpose of the C loop is to repeat the same code a number of times.

Following are the topics to be discussed:

- Types of Loops in C

Types of Loops in C

Depending upon the position of a control statement in a program, looping statement in C is classified into two types:

1. Entry controlled loop
2. Exit controlled loop

In an **entry control loop in C**, a condition is checked before executing the body of a loop. It is also called as a pre-checking loop.

In an **exit controlled loop**, a condition is checked after executing the body of a loop. It is also called as a post-checking loop.

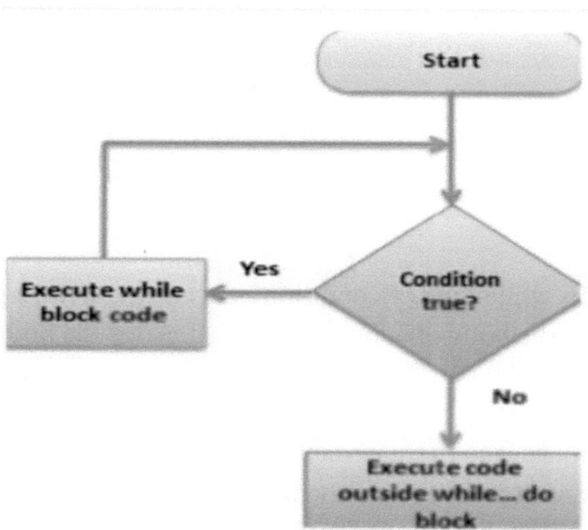

Figure:2.6

The control conditions must be well defined and specified otherwise the loop will execute an infinite number of times. The loop that does not stop executing and processes the statements number of times is called as an **infinite loop**. An infinite loop is also called as an "**Endless loop.**" Following are some characteristics of an infinite loop:

1. No termination condition is specified.
2. The specified conditions never meet.

The specified condition determines whether to execute the loop body or not.

'C' programming language provides us with three types of loop constructs:

1. The ***while*** loop
2. The ***do-while*** loop
3. The ***for*** loop

Sr. No.

Loop Type

Description

1. While Loop
In while loop, a condition is evaluated before processing a body of the loop. If a condition is true then and only then the body of a loop is executed.
2. Do-While Loop
In a do...while loop, the condition is always executed after the body of a loop. It is also called an exit-controlled loop.
3. For Loop
In a for loop, the initial value is performed only once, then the condition tests and compares the counter to a fixed value
after each iteration, stopping the for loop when false is returned.

2.61 While Loop in C

A while loop is the most straightforward looping structure. While loop syntax in C programming language is as follows:

Syntax of While Loop in C:

```
while (condition) {
    statements;
    }
```

It is an entry-controlled loop. In while loop, a condition is evaluated before processing a body of the loop. If a condition is true then and only then the body of a loop is executed. After the body of a loop is executed then control again goes back at the beginning, and the condition is checked if it is true, the same process is executed until the condition becomes false. Once the condition becomes false, the control goes out of the loop.

After exiting the loop, the control goes to the statements which are immediately after the loop. The body of a loop can contain more than one statement. If it contains only one statement, then the curly braces are not compulsory. It is a good practice though to use the curly braces even we have a single statement in the body.

In while loop, if the condition is not true, then the body of a loop will not be executed, not even once. It is different in do while loop which we will see shortly.

Following program illustrates while loop in C programming example:

```
#include<stdio.h>
#include<conio.h>
int main()
{
int num=1; //initializing the variable
while(num<=10) //while loop with condition
{
printf("%d\n",num);
num++; //incrementing operation
}
return 0;
}
```

Output:

1
2
3
4
5
6
7
8
9
10

The above program illustrates the use of while loop. In the above program, we have printed series of numbers from 1 to 10 using a while loop.

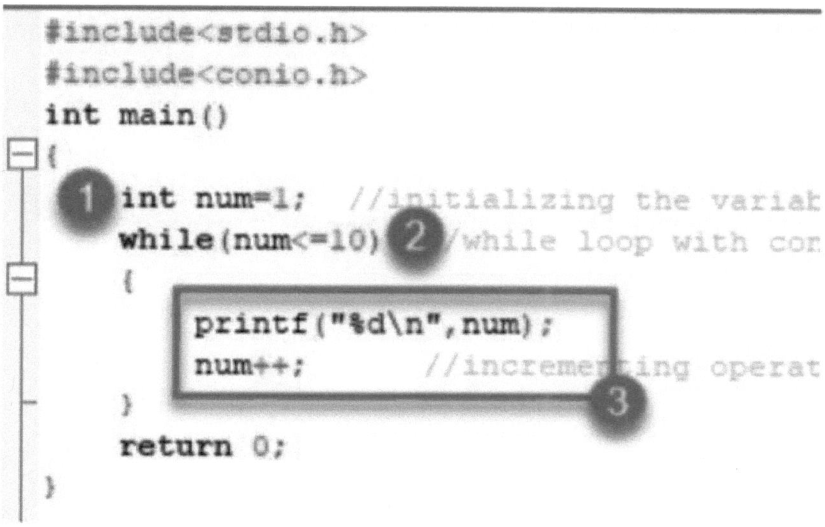

```
#include<stdio.h>
#include<conio.h>
int main()
{
    int num=1;  //initializing the variab
    while(num<=10)  //while loop with con
    {
        printf("%d\n",num);
        num++;          //incrementing operat
    }
    return 0;
}
```

While Loop in C Programming

1. We have initialized a variable called num with value 1. We are going to print from 1 to 10 hence the variable is initialized with value 1. If you want to print from 0, then assign the value 0 during initialization.
2. In a while loop, we have provided a condition (num<=10), which means the loop will execute the body until the value of num becomes 10. After that, the loop will be terminated, and control will fall outside the loop.
3. In the body of a loop, we have a print function to print our number and an increment operation to increment the value per execution of a loop. An initial value of num is 1, after the execution, it will become 2, and during the next execution, it will become 3. This process will continue until the value becomes 10 and then it will print the series on console and terminate the loop.

\n is used for formatting purposes which means the value will be printed on a new line.

2.62 Do-While loop in C

A do-while loop in C is similar to the while loop except that the condition is always executed after the body of a loop. It is also called an exit-controlled loop.

Syntax of do while loop in C programming language is as follows:

Syntax of Do-While Loop in C:

```
do {
statements
} while (expression);
```

As we saw in a while loop, the body is executed if and only if the condition is true. In some cases, we have to execute a body of the loop at least once even if the condition is false. This type of operation can be achieved by using a do-while loop.

In the do-while loop, the body of a loop is always executed at least once. After the body is executed, then it checks the condition. If the condition is true, then it will again execute the body of a loop otherwise control is transferred out of the loop.

Similar to the while loop, once the control goes out of the loop the statements which are immediately after the loop is executed.

The critical difference between the while and do-while loop is that in while loop the while is written at the beginning. In do-while loop, the while condition is written at the end and terminates with a semi-colon (;)

The following loop program in C illustrates the working of a do-while loop:

Below is a do-while loop in C example to print a table of number 2:

```
#include<stdio.h>
#include<conio.h>
int main()
{
int num=1; //initializing the variable
do //do-while loop
{
printf("%d\n",2*num);
num++; //incrementing operation
}while(num<=10);
return 0;
}
```

Output:

```
2
4
6
8
10
12
14
16
18
20
```

In the above example, we have printed multiplication table of 2 using a do-while loop. Let's see how the program print the series.

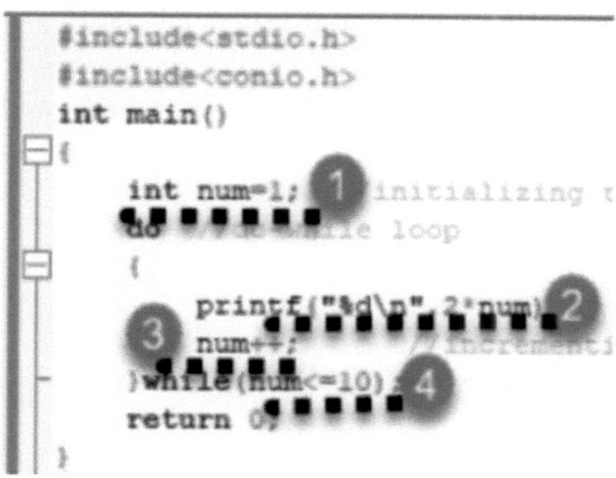

Do-While Loop in C Programming

1. First, we have initialized a variable 'num' with value 1. Then we have written a do-while loop.
2. In a loop, we have a print function that will print the series by multiplying the value of num with 2.
3. After each increment, the value of num will increase by 1, and it will be printed on the screen.
4. Initially, the value of num is 1. In a body of a loop, the print function will be executed in this way: 2*num where num=1, then 2*1=2 hence the value two will be printed. This will go on until the value of num becomes 10. After that loop will be terminated and a statement which is immediately after the loop will be executed. In this case return 0.

2.63 For loop in C

A for loop is a more efficient loop structure in 'C' programming. The general structure of for loop syntax in C is as follows:

Syntax of For Loop in C:

```
for (initial value; condition; incrementation or decrementation )
  {
  statements;
  }
```

- The initial value of the for loop is performed only once.
- The condition is a Boolean expression that tests and compares the counter to a fixed value after each iteration, stopping the for loop when false is returned.
- The incrementation/decrementation increases (or decreases) the counter by a set value.

Following program illustrates the for loop in C programming example:

```
#include<stdio.h>
int main()
{
```

```
int number;
for(number=1;number<=10;number++) //for loop to print 1-10 numbers
{
printf("%d\n",number); //to print the number
}
return 0;
}
```

Output:

1
2
3
4
5
6
7
8
9
10

The above program prints the number series from 1-10 using for loop.

```
#include<stdio.h>
int main()
{
    int number; 1
  2 for(number=1;number<=10;number++)
    {
        printf("%d\n",number) 3
    }
    return 0;
}
```

For Loop in C Programming

1. We have declared a variable of an int data type to store values.
2. In for loop, in the initialization part, we have assigned value 1 to the variable number. In the condition part, we have specified our condition and then the increment part.
3. In the body of a loop, we have a print function to print the numbers on a new line in the console. We have the value one stored in number, after the first iteration the value will be incremented, and it will become 2. Now the variable number has the value 2. The condition will be rechecked and since the condition is true loop will be executed, and it will print two on the screen. This loop will keep on executing until the value of the variable becomes 10. After that, the loop will be terminated, and a series of 1-10 will be printed on the screen.

In C, the for loop can have multiple expressions separated by commas in each part.

For example:

```
for (x = 0, y = num; x < y; i++, y--) {
statements;
}
```

Also, we can skip the initial value expression, condition and/or increment by adding a semicolon.

For example:

```
int i=0;
int max = 10;
for (; i < max; i++) {
printf("%d\n", i);
}
```

Notice that loops can also be nested where there is an outer loop and an inner loop. For each iteration of the outer loop, the inner loop repeats its entire cycle.

Consider the following example with multiple conditions in for loop, that uses nested for loop in C programming to output a multiplication table:

```
#include <stdio.h>
int main() {
int i, j;
int table = 2;
int max = 5;
for (i = 1; i <= table; i++) { // outer loop
for (j = 0; j <= max; j++) { // inner loop
printf("%d x %d = %d\n", i, j, i*j);
}
printf("\n"); /* blank line between tables */
}}
```

Output:

```
1 x 0 = 0
1 x 1 = 1
1 x 2 = 2
1 x 3 = 3
1 x 4 = 4
1 x 5 = 5
2 x 0 = 0
2 x 1 = 2
2 x 2 = 4
2 x 3 = 6
2 x 4 = 8
2 x 5 = 10
```

The nesting of for loops can be done up-to any level. The nested loops should be adequately indented to make code readable. In some versions of 'C,' the nesting is limited up to 15 loops, but some provide more.

The nested loops are mostly used in array applications which we will see in further tutorials.

2.64 Break Statement in C

The break statement is used mainly in in the switch statement. It is also useful for immediately stopping a loop.

We consider the following program which introduces a break to exit a while loop:

```
#include <stdio.h>
int main() {
int num = 5;
while (num > 0) {
if (num == 3)
break;
printf("%d\n", num);
num--;
}}
```

Output:

5

4

2.65 Continue Statement in C

When you want to skip to the next iteration but remain in the loop, you should use the continue statement.

For example:

```
#include <stdio.h>
int main() {
int nb = 7;
while (nb > 0) {
nb--;
if (nb == 5)
continue;
printf("%d\n", nb);
}}
```

Output:

6

4

3

2

1

So, the value 5 is skipped.

2.66 Which loop to Select?

Selection of a loop is always a tough task for a programmer, to select a loop do the following steps:

- Analyse the problem and check whether it requires a pre-test or a post-test loop.
- If pre-test is required, use a while or for a loop.
- If post-test is required, use a do-while loop.

Summary

- Define loop in C: A Loop is one of the key concepts in any Programming language. Loops in C language are implemented using conditional statements.
- A block of loop control statements in C are executed for number of times until the condition becomes false.
- Loops in C programming are of 2 types: entry-controlled and exit-controlled.
- List various loop control instructions in C: C programming provides us 1) while 2) do-while and 3) for loop control instructions.
- For and while loop C programming are entry-controlled loops in C language.
- Do-while is an exit control loop in C.

Programs for practice:
1. Finding roots of a quadratic equation
Description:
The standard form of a quadratic equation is:
ax2 + bx + c = 0, where
a, b and c are real numbers and
a != 0
The term b^2- 4ac is known as the discriminant of a quadratic equation. It tells the nature of the roots.

- If the discriminant is greater than 0, the roots are real and different.
- If the discriminant is equal to 0, the roots are real and equal.
- If the discriminant is less than 0, the roots are complex and different.

If the discriminant > 0,

$$root1 = \frac{-b + \sqrt{(b^2 - 4ac)}}{2a}$$

$$root2 = \frac{-b - \sqrt{(b^2 - 4ac)}}{2a}$$

If the discriminant = 0,

$$root1 = root2 = \frac{-b}{2a}$$

If the discriminant < 0,

$$root1 = \frac{-b}{2a} + \frac{i\sqrt{-(b^2 - 4ac)}}{2a}$$

$$root2 = \frac{-b}{2a} - \frac{i\sqrt{-(b^2 - 4ac)}}{2a}$$

Program:

```
#include <math.h>
#include <stdio.h>
int main() {
double a, b, c, discriminant, root1, root2, realPart, imagPart;
```

```
printf("Enter coefficients a, b and c: ");
scanf("%lf %lf %lf", &a, &b, &c);
discriminant = b * b - 4 * a * c;
// condition for real and different roots
if (discriminant > 0) {
root1 = (-b + sqrt(discriminant)) / (2 * a);
root2 = (-b - sqrt(discriminant)) / (2 * a);
printf("root1 = %.2lf and root2 = %.2lf", root1, root2);
}
// condition for real and equal roots
else if (discriminant == 0) {
root1 = root2 = -b / (2 * a);
printf("root1 = root2 = %.2lf;", root1);
}
// if roots are not real
else {
realPart = -b / (2 * a);
imagPart = sqrt(-discriminant) / (2 * a);
printf("root1 = %.2lf+%.2lfi and root2 = %.2f-%.2fi", realPart, imagPart, realPart, imagPart);
}
return 0;
}
```

Sample Output:

```
Enter coefficients a, b and c: 2.3
4
5.6
root1 = -0.87+1.30i and root2 = -0.87-1.30i
```

2. Computation of Binomial Coefficients:

Description:

$$\binom{n}{k} = \frac{n!}{k!(n-k)!} \quad \text{2.1:}$$

2.1: Formula for binomial coefficient

Program:

```
#include<stdio.h>
long int fact(int a);
void main()
{
long int n,k,nck;
printf("Enter the values of n and r \n");
scanf("%ld%ld",&n,&r);
ncr=fact(n)/((fact(n-k))*(fact(k)));
printf("nck=%d\n",nck);
}
```

```
long int fact(int a)
{
if(a==0)
return 1;
else
return a*fact(a-1);
}
```

Sample Output

Run 1	Run 2
Enter the values of n and k	Enter the values of n and k
5	6
2	4
ncr=10	ncr=15

Enter Caption

3. Plotting orPascal's Triangle:

Description:

Pascal's triangle is one of the classic example taught to engineering students. It has many interpretations. One of the famous is its use with binomial equations.

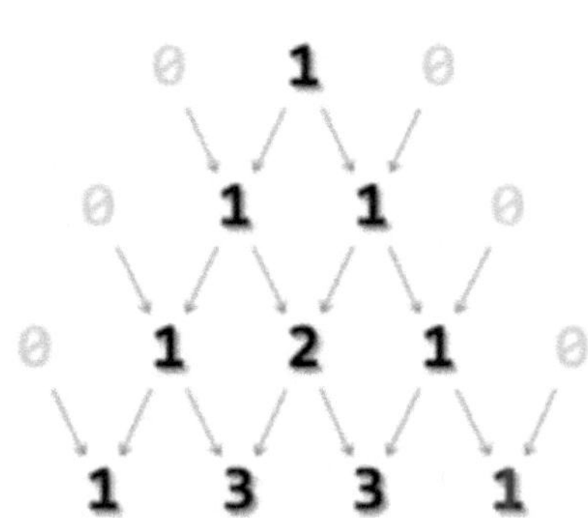

All values outside the triangle are considered zero (0). The first row is 0 1 0 whereas only 1 acquire a space in Pascal's triangle, 0s are invisible. Second row is acquired by adding (0+1) and (1+0). The output is sandwiched between two zeroes. The process continues till the required level is achieved.

Program:

```
#include <stdio.h>
int main()
{
int rows, coef = 1, space, i, j;
printf("Enter the number of rows: ");
scanf("%d", &rows);
for (i = 0; i < rows; i++)
```

```
{
for (space = 1; space <= rows - i; space++)
printf("");
for (j = 0; j <= i; j++) {
if (j == 0 || i == 0)
coef = 1;
else
coef = coef * (i - j + 1) / j;
printf("%4d", coef);
}
printf("\n");
}
return 0;
}
```

CHAPTER THREE

Module-3 ARRAYS

3.1 Array:

An array in C can be defined as "a collection of data items of the same data type which are stored in consecutive memory locations and referred by the common name".

Real time example: A biscuit packet which is a collection of biscuits of same type wrapped in a packet.

The Variable allows us to store a single value at a time, what if we want to store roll no. of 100 students? For this task, we have to declare 100 variables, and then assign values to each of them.

What if there are 10000 students or more? As you can see declaring that many variables for a single entity (i.e. student) are not a good idea.

Concept of an array:

Suppose, you want to store salary of 100 employees. You can store salaries of all employees by creating 100 variable of float data type individually like employeeSalary1, employeeSalary2, employeeSalary3 employeeSalary100.

This is very tedious, time-consuming and difficult to maintain a method of storing 100 salaries.

In this type of situation, C language provides support for array data structure, which solves the problem of storing N similar data. We can declare a float array of length 100 to store salaries of 100 employees.

It is a linear and homogeneous data structure. Linear data structure stores its individual data elements in sequential order in the memory. Homogenous means all the individual data elements are of same data type.

The data type of the elements may be any valid data type like char, int or float.

The elements of an array in C share the same variable name but each element has a different index number known as a subscript. i.e. we can access the individual elements of an array using index or subscript.

Array declaration tells to Compiler about Type of the array, Name of the Array and Size of array.

The general **syntax** for declaring an array is as follows:

<data_type> array_name[size1][size2].....[sizen].

where data_type can be basic data type or structure.

[size1][size2].....[sizen] specify dimension of an array.

For Example:

int age[100]; double employee[100]; float volume[80][20][40];

For the above problem, we can take an array variable age[100] of type int. The size of this array variable is 100 so it is capable of storing 100 integer values.

The individual elements of this array are age[0], age[1], age[2],age[3], age[4], age[98], age[99].

In C the subscripts or index start from zero, so age[0] is the first element, age [1] is the second element of an array and so on.

Types of Array:

In C, there are three types of array namely, One Dimension Array, Two Dimensional Array and Multi-Dimensional Array.

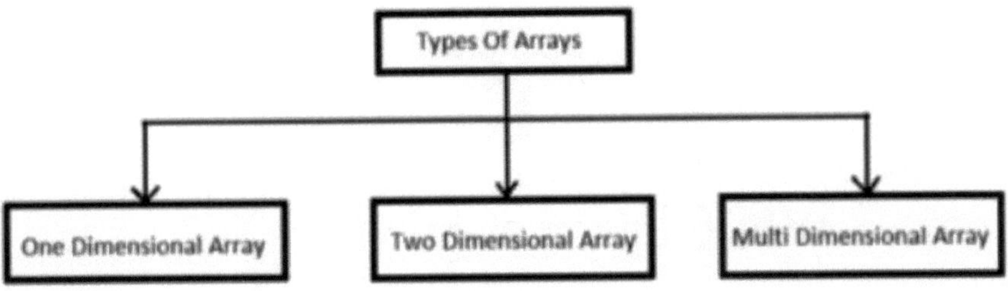

Figure: 3.1

1. One Dimensional Array

A one-dimensional array has one index or subscript. One Dimensional (1D) array is an array which is represented either in one row or in one column.

The one-dimensional arrays are known as vectors.

In other words, it can be represented as in a single dimension-width or height as shown in the below figure:

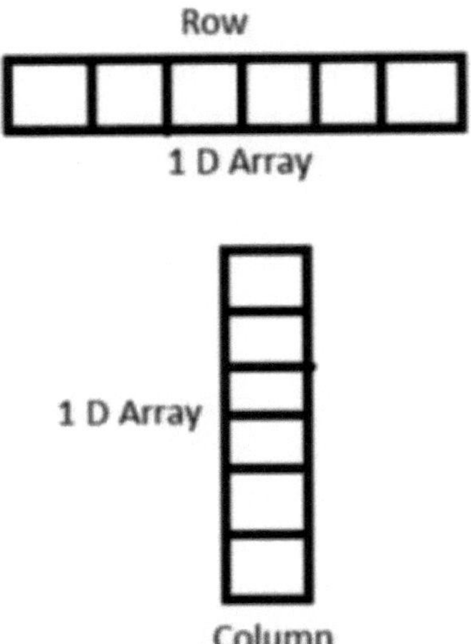

2. Two Dimensional Array

Two Dimensional (2D) array is a fixed-length, homogeneous data type, row and column-based data structure which is used to store similar data type element in a row and column-based structure.

A two-dimensional array is referred to as a matrix or a table. A matrix has two subscripts, one denotes the row and another denotes the column.

In other words, a two-dimensional array is an array of a one-dimensional array.

The general **syntax** for declaration of a 2D array is given below:

data_type array_name[row] [column];

Where data_type specifies the data type of the array. array_name specifies the name of the array, row specifies the number of rows in the array and column specifies the number of columns in the array.

The total number of elements that can be stored in a two array can be calculated by multiplying the size of all the dimensions.

For example :The array int x[10][20] can store total (10*20) = 200 elements.

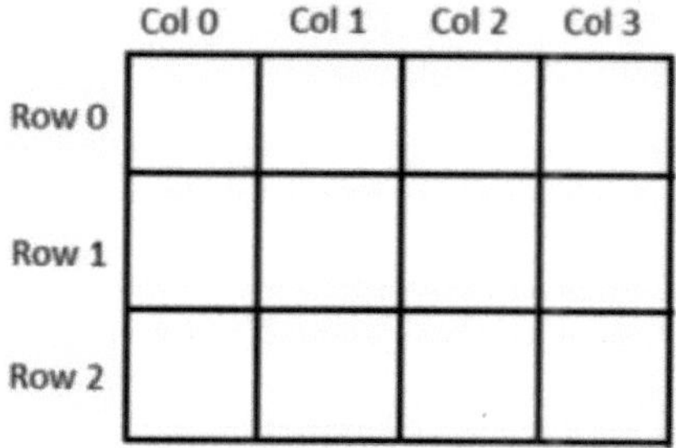

3.2 Character array &strings:

String is a sequence or collection of characters that are considered as a single data item and terminated by a null character '\0'. Remember that the C language does not support strings as a data type. A **string** is actually a one-dimensional array of characters in C language. These are often used to create meaningful and readable programs.

For example: The string "home" contains 5 characters including the '\0'character which is automatically added by the compiler at the end of the string.

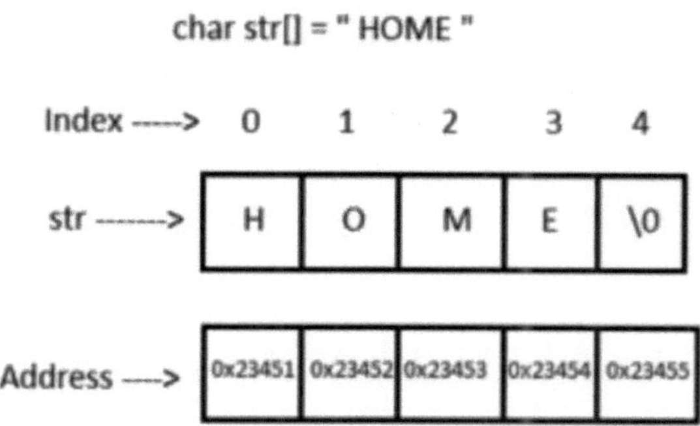

3.3 Declaring and Initializing a string variables:

// valid
char name[13] = "StudyTonight";
char name[10] = {'c','o','d','e','\0'};

3.4 String Handling Functions:

Language supports a large number of string handling functions that can be used to carry out many of the string manipulations. These functions are packaged in the **string.h** library. Hence, you must include **string.h** header file in your programs to use these functions.

The following are the most commonly used string handling functions.

Method	Description
strcat()	It is used to concatenate(combine) two strings
strlen()	It is used to show the length of a string
strrev()	It is used to show the reverse of a string
strcpy()	Copies one string into another
strcmp()	It is used to compare two string

3.41 Strcat() function in C:

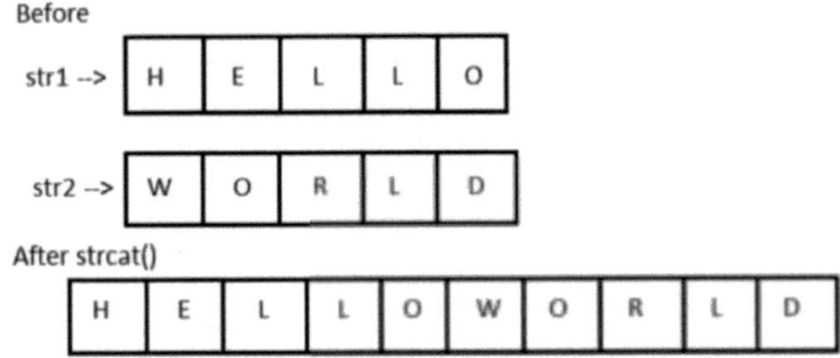

Syntax:
strcat("str1","str2");
Example:
strcat("computer", "science");
Output:
computerscience

3.42 strlen() and strcmp() function:

Strlen() will return the length of the string passed to it and strcmp() will return the ASCII difference between first unmatching character of two strings.

Syntax:
strlen("string");

```
strcmp("str1","str2")
Example:
int j = strlen("computer");
int i=strcmp("study ", "computer");
printf("%d",j);
output:
8
```

3.43 strcpy() function:

It copies the second string argument to the first string argument.

Syntax:

```
char* strcpy(char* destination, const char* source);
```

Example:

```
#include<stdio.h>
#include<string.h>
int main()
{
char s1[50], s2[50];
strcpy(s1, "CSE");
strcpy(s2, s1);
printf("%s\n", s2);
return(0);
}
```

Output:

CSE

3.44 strrev() **function:**

It is used to reverse the given string expression.

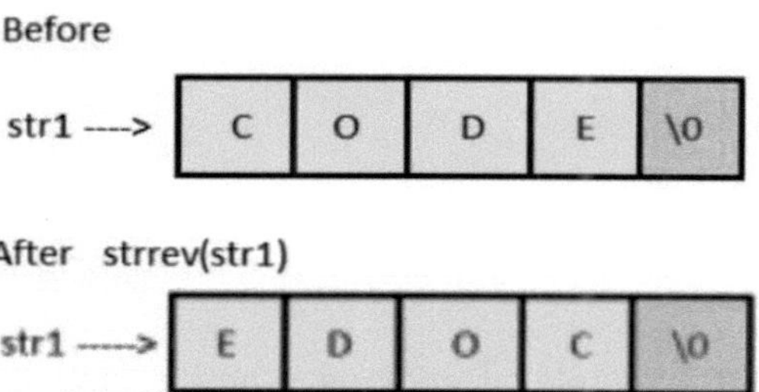

Synatx:

```
char *strrev(char *string);
```

Example 1:

```
#include <stdio.h>
int main()
{
char s1[50];
printf("Enter your string: ");
gets(s1);
```

```
printf("\nYour reverse string is: %s",strrev(s1));
return(0);
}
```

Output:

Enter your string: cse

Your reverse string is: ese

Example 2:

```
#include<stdio.h>
#include<string.h>
int main()
{
charname[30]="Hello";
printf("String before strrev( ) : %s\n",name);
printf("String after strrev( ) : %s",strrev(name));
return 0;
}
```

OUTPUT:

String before strrev( ) : Hello

String after strrev( ) : olleH

3.5 Basic Algorithm:

--Searching Algorithms: Binary search, linear search

--Sorting Algorithms: Bubble sort, Selection sort

Algorithm:

The word Algorithm means "a process or set of rules to be followed in calculations or other problem-solving operations". Therefore Algorithm refers to a set of rules/instructions/procedures that step-by-step define how a work is to be executed, in order to get the expected results.

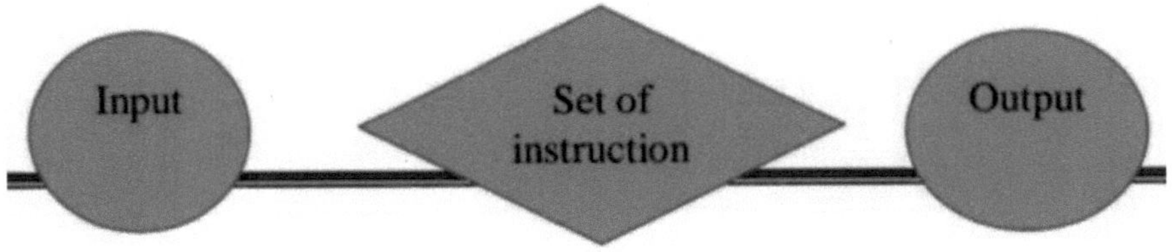

Fig 3.1: Representation of an Algorithm

It can be understood by taking an example of cooking a new recipe. To cook a new recipe, one reads the instructions and steps and execute them one by one, in the given sequence. The result thus obtained is the new dish cooked perfectly. Similarly, algorithms help to do a task in programming to get the expected output. The Algorithm designed are language-independent, i.e. they are just plain instructions that can be implemented in any language, and yet the output will be the same, as expected.

3.51 Binary search algorithm:

Search algorithm are utilised to find or locate a given element in the specified list.

Binary Search:

Search a sorted array by repeatedly dividing the search interval in half. Begin with an interval covering the whole array. If the value of the search key is less than the item in the middle of the interval, narrow the interval to the lower half. Otherwise, narrow it to the upper half. Repeatedly check until the value is found or the interval is empty.

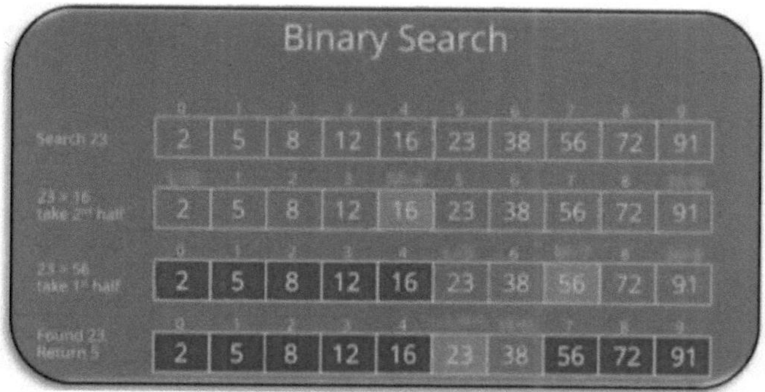

Steps:

- Compare x with the middle element.
- If x matches with the middle element, we return the mid index.
- Else If x is greater than the mid element, then x can only lie in the right half sub array after the mid element. So we recur for the right half.
- Else (x is smaller) recur for the left half.

Program:

```
#include <stdio.h>
int main()
{
int c,first,last,middle,n,search,array[100];
printf("Enter number of elements\n");
scanf("%d",&n);
printf("Enter %d integers\n",n);
for(c=0;c<n;c++)
scanf("%d",&array[c]);
printf("Enter value to find\n");
scanf("%d",&search);
first=0;
last=n-1;
middle=(first+last)/2;
while(first<=last)
{
if(array[middle]<search)
first=middle+1;
else if(array[middle]==search){
printf("%d found at location %d.\n",search,middle+1);
break;
}
else
last=middle-1;
middle=(first+last)/2;
}
if(first>last)
```

```
printf("Not found! %d isn't present in the list.\n",search);
    return 0;
}
```

3.52Linear Search:

linear search, searching is performed from first element to last element in a sequential order i.e, one after other in order.

Steps:

A simple approach is to do a **linear search**, i.e

- Start from the leftmost element of arr[] and one by one compare x with each element of arr[]
- If x matches with an element, return the index.
- If x doesn't match with any of elements, return -1.

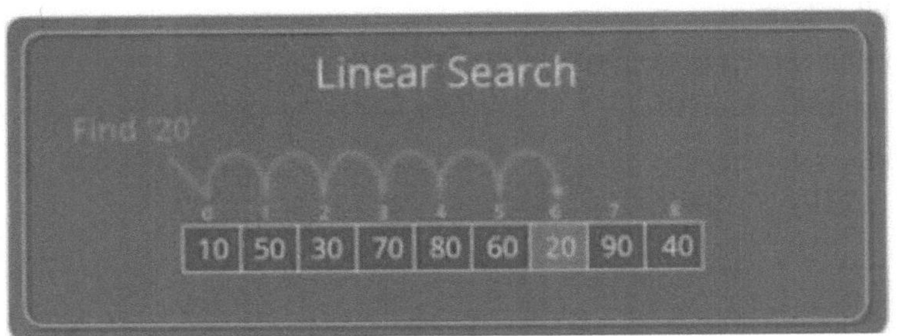

Example:

Given an array arr[] of n elements, write a function to search a given element x in arr[].

Examples:

Input: arr[] = {10, 20, 80, 30, 60, 50,
110, 100, 130, 170}
x = 110;

Output: 6

Element x is present at index 6

Input: arr[] = {10, 20, 80, 30, 60, 50,
110, 100, 130, 170}
x = 175;

Output: -1

Element x is not present in arr[].

Program:

```
#include<stdio.h>
Void main ()
{
int a[10]={10,23,40,1,2,0,14,13,50,9};
int item,i,flag;
printf("\nEnter Item to be searched\n");
scanf("%d",&item);
for(i=0;i<10;i++)
{
if(a[i]==item)
```

```
{
flag=i+1;
break;
}
else
flag=0;
}
if(flag!=0)
{
printf("\nItem found at location %d\n",flag);
}
else
{
printf("\nItem not found\n");
}
}
```

3.53Sorting Algorithms:

Sorting algorithms are used for ordering elements in the given list (either in ascending or descending order).

Bubble sort:

Steps:

Suppose we are trying to sort the elements in **ascending order**.

First Iteration (Compare and Swap)

1. Starting from the first index, compare the first and the second elements.
2. If the first element is greater than the second element, they are swapped.
3. Now, compare the second and the third elements. Swap them if they are not in order.
4. The above process goes on until the last element.

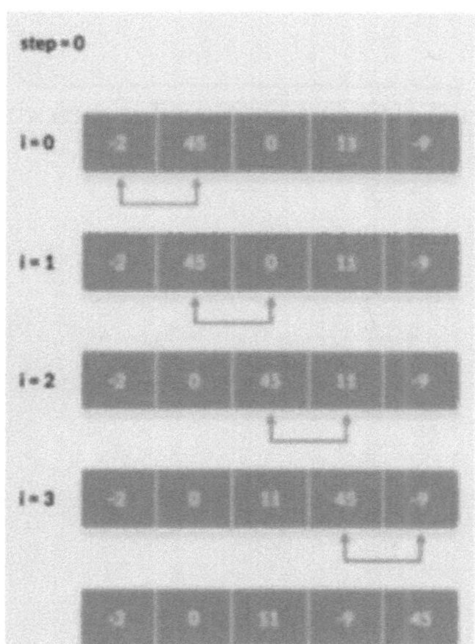

2. Remaining Iteration

The same process goes on for the remaining iterations.

After each iteration, the largest element among the unsorted elements is placed at the end.

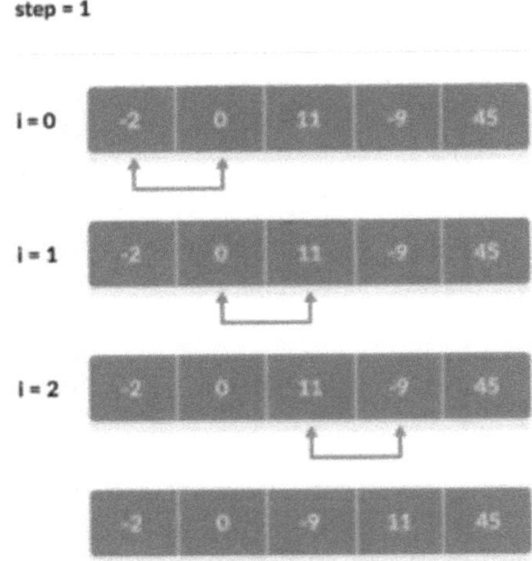

In each iteration, the comparison takes place up to the last unsorted element.

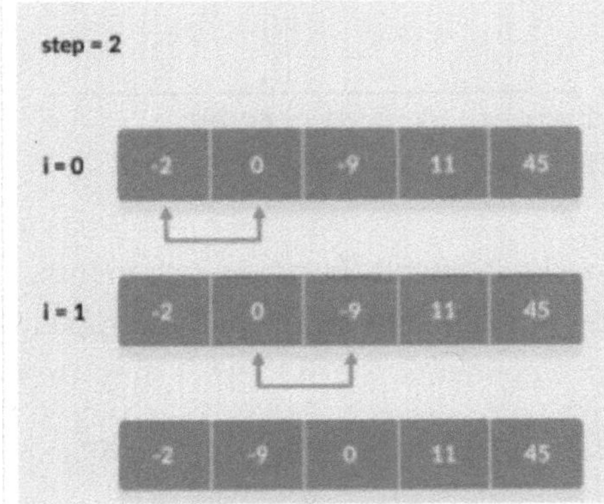

The array is sorted when all the unsorted elements are placed at their correct positions.

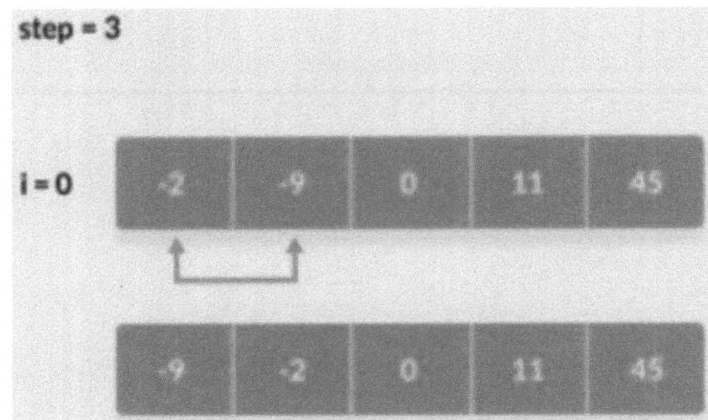

Program:

```
#include <stdio.h>
int main()
```

```
{
int array[100],n,c,d,swap;
printf("Enter number of elements\n");
scanf("%d",&n);
printf("Enter %d integers\n",n);
for(c=0;c<n;c++)
scanf("%d",&array[c]);
for(c=0;c<n-1;c++)
{
for(d=0;d<n-c-1;d++)
{
if(array[d]>array[d+1])/* For decreasing order use '<' instead of '>' */
{
swap=array[d];
array[d]=array[d+1];
array[d+1]=swap;
}
}
}
printf("Sorted list in ascending order:\n");
for(c=0;c<n;c++)
printf("%d\n",array[c]);
return 0;
}
```

3.54Selection Sort:

Steps:

The selection sort algorithm sorts an array by repeatedly finding the minimum element (considering ascending order) from unsorted part and putting it at the beginning. The algorithm maintains two subarrays in a given array.

- The subarray which is already sorted.
- Remaining subarray which is unsorted.

In every iteration of selection sort, the minimum element (considering ascending order) from the unsorted subarray is picked and moved to the sorted subarray.

Example:

arr[] = 64 25 12 22 11
// Find the minimum element in arr[0...4]
// and place it at beginning
11 25 12 22 64
// Find the minimum element in arr[1...4]
// and place it at beginning of arr[1...4]
11 **12** 25 22 64
// Find the minimum element in arr[2...4]
// and place it at beginning of arr[2...4]
11 12 **22** 25 64
// Find the minimum element in arr[3...4]
// and place it at beginning of arr[3...4]
11 12 22 **25** 64

Program:

```
#include<stdio.h>
int main(){
/* Here i & j for loop counters, temp for swapping,
* Count for total number of elements, number [] to
* store the input numbers in array. You can increase
* or decrease the size of number array as per requirement
*/
int i, j, count, temp, number[25];
printf("How many numbers u are going to enter?: ");
scanf("%d",&count);
printf("Enter %d elements: ", count);
// Loop to get the elements stored in array
for(i=0;i<count;i++)
scanf("%d",&number[i]);
// Logic of selection sort algorithm
for(i=0;i<count;i++){
for(j=i+1;j<count;j++){
if(number[i]>number[j]){
temp=number[i];
number[i]=number[j];
number[j]=temp;
}
}
}
printf("Sorted elements: ");
for(i=0;i<count;i++)
printf(" %d",number[i]);
return 0;
}
```

CHAPTER FOUR

Module-4 FUNCTION

4.1 Functions:

Definition:

A function is a set of statements that take inputs, do some specific computation and produces output.The idea is to put some commonly or repeatedly done task together and make a function so that instead of writing the same code again and again for different inputs, we can call the function.

Syntax:

return_type function_name([arg1_type arg1_name, ...]) { code/function body }

where:

Return Type- A function may return a value. The return_type is the data type of the value the function returns. Some functions perform the desired operations without returning a value. In this case, the return_type is the keyword void.

Function Name – This is the actual name of the function. The function name and the parameter list together constitute the function signature.

Arguments – A parameter is like a placeholder. When a function is invoked, you pass a value to the parameter. This value is referred to as actual parameter or argument. The parameter list refers to the type, order, and number of the parameters of a function. Parameters are optional; that is, a function may contain no parameters.

Function Body – The function body contains a collection of statements that define what the function does.

Example:

```
#include <stdio.h>
// An example function that takes two parameters 'x' and 'y'
// as input and returns max of two input numbers
int max(int x, int y)
{
if (x > y)
return x;
else
return y;
}
// main function that doesn't receive any parameter and
// returns integer.
int main()
{
int a = 10, b = 20;
// Calling above function to find max of 'a' and 'b'
int m = max(a, b);
printf("m is %d", m);
return 0;
}
```

Application:

- C functions are used to avoid rewriting same logic/code again and again in a program.
- There is no limit in calling C functions to make use of same functionality wherever required.
- We can call functions any number of times in a program and from any place in a program.
- Reusability is the main achievement of C functions.

Types of Functions:
There are two types of functions in C programming:

1. **Library Functions or Inbuilt- functions:** These are the functions which are declared in the C header files such as scanf(), printf(), gets(), puts() etc. These functions are already defined in the header files. Users need not to recode library functions.
2. **User-defined functions:** are the functions which are created by the C programmer, so that he/she can use it many times. It reduces the complexity of a big program and optimizes the code.

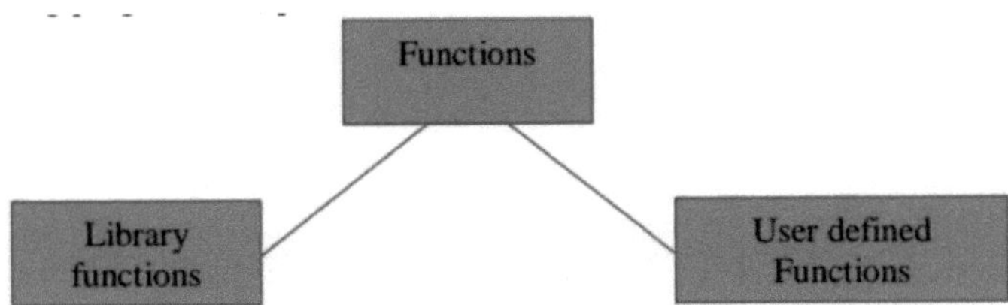

Fig 4.1: Classification of functions

4.11 Library Functions or Inbuilt- functions: These are the functions which are declared in the C header files such as scanf(), printf(), gets(), puts() etc. These functions are already defined in the header files. Users need not to recode library functions.

We include the header files in our C program by using **#include<filename.h>**. Whenever the program is run and executed, the related files are included in the C program.

Header File Functions

Some of the header file functions are as follows –

- **stdio.h** – It is a standard i/o header file in which Input/output functions are declared
- **conio.h** – This is a console input/output header file.
- **string.h** – All string related functions are in this header file.
- **stdlib.h** – This file contains common functions which are used in the C programs.
- **math.h** – All functions related to mathematics are in this header file.
- **time.h** – This file contains time and clock related functions. Built functions in stdio.h

Built functions in stdio.h

Let's see what are the built functions present in stdio.h library function.

Sl.No	Function & Description
1	printf() This function is used to print the all char, int, float, string etc., values onto the output screen.
2	scanf() This function is used to read data from keyboard.
3	getc() It reads character from file.
4	gets() It reads line from keyboard.
5	getchar() It reads character from keyboard.
6	puts() It writes line to o/p screen.
24	SEEK_SET Moves file pointer at the beginning of the file.
25	SEEK_CUR Moves file pointer at given location.
26	SEEK_END Moves file pointer at the end of file.
27	ftell() Gives current position of file pointer.
28	rewind() Moves file pointer to the beginning of the file.
29	putc() Writes a character to file.
30	sprint() Writes formatted output to string.
31	sscanf() Reads formatted input from a string.
32	remove() Deletes a file.
33	flush() Flushes a file.

Example:

```
#include <stdio.h>
#include <math.h>
int main()
{
```

```
float num, root;
printf("Enter a number: ");
scanf("%f", &num);
// Computes the square root of num and stores in root.
root = sqrt(num);
printf("Square root of %f = %f", num, root);
return 0;
}
```

4.12 User-defined functions: are the functions which are created by the C programmer, so that he/she can use it many times. It reduces the complexity of a big program and optimizes the code.

Here is an example to add two integers. To perform this task, we have created an user-defined addNumbers().

Example:

```
#include <stdio.h>
int addNumbers(int a, int b); // function prototype
int main()
{
int n1,n2,sum;
printf("Enters two numbers: ");
scanf("%d %d",&n1,&n2);
sum = addNumbers(n1, n2); // function call
printf("sum = %d",sum);
return 0;
}
int addNumbers(int a, int b) // function definition
{
int result;
result = a+b;
return result; } // return statement
```

4.13 Function prototype:

A function prototype is simply the declaration of a function that specifies function's name, parameters and return type. It doesn't contain function body.

A function prototype gives information to the compiler that the function may later be used in the program.

Syntax of function prototype:

returnType functionName(type1 argument1, type2 argument2, ...);

In the above example,int addNumbers(int a, int b);is the function prototype which provides the following information to the compiler:

1. name of the function is addNumbers()
2. return type of the function is int
3. two arguments of type int are passed to the function

The function prototype is not needed if the user-defined function is defined before the main()function.

4.14 Calling a function:

Control of the program is transferred to the user-defined function by calling it.

Syntax of function call:

functionName(argument1, argument2, ...);

In the above example, the function call is made using addNumbers(n1, n2); statement inside the main() function.

4.15 Function definition:

Function definition contains the block of code to perform a specific task. In our example, adding two numbers and returning it.

```
Syntax of function definition:
returnType functionName(type1 argument1, type2 argument2, ...)
{
//body of the function
}
```

4.16 Return Statement:

The return statement terminates the execution of a function and returns a value to the calling function. The program control is transferred to the calling function after the return statement.In the above example, the value of the *result* variable is returned to the main function. The *sum* variable in the main() function is assigned this value.

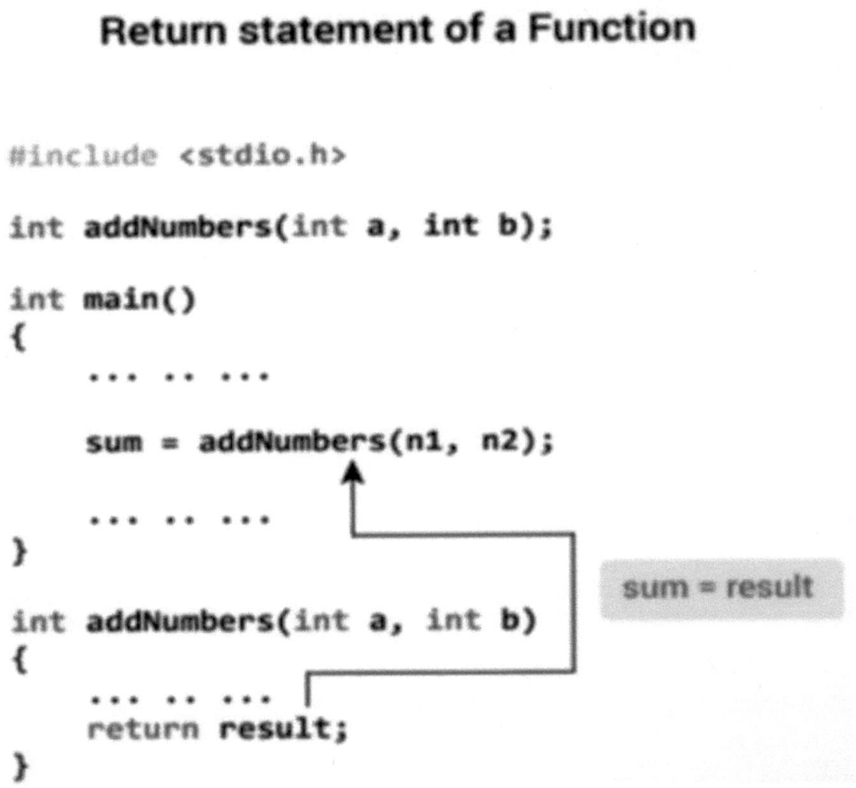

Return statement of a Function

```
#include <stdio.h>

int addNumbers(int a, int b);

int main()
{
    ... .. ...

    sum = addNumbers(n1, n2);

    ... .. ...
}

int addNumbers(int a, int b)
{
    ... .. ...
    return result;
}
```


Syntax of return statement:

return (expression);

For example:

return a;

return (a+b);

The type of value returned from the function and the return type specified in the function prototype and function definition must match.

4.2 Local variables & global variables:

4.21 Variable:

Variable is a name assign to a storage area that the program can manipulate. A variable type determines the size and layout of the variable's memory.It also determines the range of values which need to be stored inside that memory and nature of operations that can be applied to that variable.Real time example: Variable is just like a name given to a person. Once a name is assigned, it becomes the id of the person.

Scope ofVariables:

The scope of the variable is simply lifetime of a variable. It is block of code under which a variable is applicable or alive. For example:

```
function foo(){
var x;
}
```

You declare a variable "x" inside a function "foo." The scope of that variable remains inside that function it can't be used outside of that function.

There are three places where variables you can declare variable programming language:

- Inside a function or a block: Local variables
- Outside of all functions: Global variables
- In the definition of function parameters: Formal parameter

4.22 KEY DIFFERENCE:

- Local variable is declared inside a function whereas Global variable is declared outside the function.
- Local variables are created when the function has started execution and is lost when the function terminates, on the other hand, Global variable is created as execution starts and is lost when the program ends.
- Local variable doesn't provide data sharing whereas Global variable provides data sharing.
- Local variables are stored on the stack whereas the Global variable are stored on a fixed location decided by the compiler.
- Parameters passing is required for local variables whereas it is not necessary for a global variable

4.23 Local Variable:

Local Variable is defined as a type of variable declared within programming block or subroutines. It can only be used inside the subroutine or code block in which it is declared. The local variable exists until the block of the function is under execution. After that, it will be destroyed automatically.

Real-time example: Local variable is similar to regional language which is understood within a specific region but not outside the region.

Example of Local Variable

```
public int add(){
int a =4;
int b=5;
return a+b;
}
```

Here, ‘a’ and ‘b’ are local variables

4.24 Global Variable:

A **Global Variable** in the program is a variable defined outside the subroutine or function. It has a global scope means it holds its value throughout the lifetime of the program.

Real time example: Global variable is similar to English language which is understood at every corner of the world.

Example:

```
int a =4;
```

```
int b=5;
public int add(){
return a+b;
}
```

Here, 'a' and 'b' are global variables.

Here, are some fundamental differences between Local and Global variables.

Parameter	Local	Global
Scope	It is declared inside a function.	It is declared outside the function.
Value	If it is not initialized, a garbage value is stored	If it is not initialized zero is stored as default.
Lifetime	It is created when the function starts execution and lost when the functions terminate.	It is created before the program's global execution starts and lost when the program terminates.
Data sharing	Data sharing is not possible as data of the local variable can be accessed by only one function.	Data sharing is possible as multiple functions can access the same global variable.
Parameters	Parameters passing is required for local variables to access the value in other function	Parameters passing is not necessary for a global variable as it is visible throughout the program
Modification of variable value	When the value of the local variable is modified in one function, the changes are not visible in another function.	When the value of the global variable is modified in one function changes are visible in the rest of the program.
Accessed by	Local variables can be accessed with the help of statements, inside a function in which they are declared.	You can access global variables by any statement in the program.
Memory storage	It is stored on the stack unless specified.	It is stored on a fixed location decided by the compiler.

Advantages of using Global variables:

- You can access the global variable from all the functions or modules in a program
- You only require to declare global variable single time outside the modules.
- It is ideally used for storing "constants" as it helps you keep the consistency.
- A Global variable is useful when multiple functions are accessing the same data.

Advantages of using Local Variables:

- The use of local variables offer a guarantee that the values of variables will remain intact while the task is running
- If several tasks change a single variable that is running simultaneously, then the result may be unpredictable. But declaring it as local variable solves this issue as each task will create its own instance of the local variable.
- You can give local variables the same name in different functions because they are only recognized by the function they are declared in.
- Local variables are deleted as soon as any function is over and release the memory space which it occupies.

Disadvantages of using Global Variables:

- If too many variables are declared as global, then they remain in the memory till program execution is completed. This can cause of Out of Memory issue.
- Data can be modified by any function. Any statement written in the program can change the value of the global variable. This may give unpredictable results in multi-tasking environments.
- If global variables are discontinued due to code refactoring, you will need to change all the modules where they are called.

Disadvantages of using Local Variables:

- The debugging process of a local variable is quite tricky (Compleex).
- Common data required to pass repeatedly as data sharing is not possible between modules.
- They have a very limited scope.

4.3 Types of functions based on parameters:

In real-time, a function in C may define with or without parameters, and a function may or may not return a value. It entirely depends upon the user requirement. In C Programming, as per our requirement, we can define the User-defined functions in multiple ways. The following are a list of available types of Functions in C

1. Function with no argument and no Return value
2. Function with no argument and with a Return value
3. Function with argument and No Return value
4. Function with argument and Return value

From the above, 1 and 3 types do not return any value when we call the function. So, We use the void return type while defining the function.

When we call the functions 2 and 4 types, they will return some value. That's why we have to use the appropriate data type (int, float, double, etc.) as a return type while defining the function. We use the return keyword inside the function to return some value when we call the function from the main() function or any sub-functions.

4.31 Types of Functions in C Programming

The following examples will explain to you the available function types in C programming.

C Function with No argument and No Return value.In this method, we won't pass any arguments to the function while defining, declaring, or calling the function. This type of functions in C will not return any value when we call the function from main() or any sub-function. When we are not expecting any return value, but we need some statements to print as output. Then, this type of function in C is very useful.

C Function with No argument and No Return value Example

In these types of Functions in C program, We are going to calculate the Sum of 2 integer values and print the output from the user-defined function itself.

```
/* Function with No argument and No Return value Example */
#include<stdio.h>
// Function Declaration
void Addition();
void main()
{
printf("\n ............ \n");
Addition();
}
void Addition()
{
int Sum, a = 10, b = 20;
Sum = a + b;
printf("\n Sum of a = %d and b = %d is = %d", a, b, Sum);
}
```

Output:

Sum of a=10 and b=20 is =30

Within these types of Functions in C example, If you observe the main() function, We haven't passed any arguments /parameters to the function Addition()

Within the Addition function, we declared the integer variables of the sum, a, b, and we assigned 10 to a and 20 to b.

In the next C Programming line, we calculate the sum using Arithmetic operator(+)

Sum = a + b

= 10 + 20

= 30

Below printf statement is used to print the output.

`printf("\n Sum of a = %d and b = %d is = %d", a, b, Sum);`

Whenever we call the Addition () function, it will print the same output because the values of a and b are fixed inside the function.

4.32 C Function with no argument and with Return value

In this method, We won't pass any arguments to the function while defining, declaring, or calling the function. This type of function will return some value when we call the function from main() or any sub function.

The Data Type of the return value will depend upon the return type of function declaration. For instance, if the return type is int then return value will be int.

Function with No arguments and with Return value

Example

In this program, we are going to calculate the multiplication of 2 integer values using the user-defined function without arguments and return keyword.

```
#include<stdio.h>
int Multiplication();
int main()
{
int Multi;
Multi = Multiplication();
printf("\n Multiplication of a and b is = %d \n", Multi );
return 0;
}
int Multiplication()
{
int Multi, a = 20, b = 40;
Multi = a * b;
return Multi;
}
```

Output:

Multiplication of a and b is = 800

If you observe the main() function, we declared the integer variable Multi. We assigned it to the return value of the Multiplication () function. Because user-defined function also returns integer value only.

```
Multi = Multiplication();
```

We haven't passed any arguments /parameters to the function Multiplication()

In the next line, the printf statement is to print the output

```
printf("\n Multiplication of a and b is = %d \n", Multi);
```

Whenever we call the Multiplication () function, it will print the above statement.

Within the Multiplication () function, we declared the integer variables of Multi, a, b, and we assigned 20 to a and 40 to b.

In the next line, we Multiplied both a and b using Arithmetic operator(*)

Multi = a * b

= 20 * 40

= 800

Whenever we call the Multiplication () function, it prints the same output because the values of a and b are the same inside the function.

4.33 C Function with argument and No Return value

If you observe the above two methods, No matter how many times you executive, it will give the same output. We don't have any control over the values of the variables a and b because they are fixed values.

In real-time, we mostly deal with dynamic data means we have to allow the user to enter his own values rather than fixed ones.

This method allows us to pass the arguments to the function while calling the function. But, this type of function will not return any value when we call the function from main () or any sub function.

If we want to allow the user to pass his data to the function arguments, but we are not expecting any return value, this type of function is very useful.

Function with argument and No Return value Example

These Types of Functions in C program allows the user to enter 2 integer values. Next, We are going to pass those values to the user-defined function to calculate the sum.

```
#include<stdio.h>
void Addition(int, int);
void main()
{
int a, b;
printf("\n Please Enter two integer values \n");
scanf("%d %d",&a, &b);
//Calling the function with dynamic values
Addition(a, b);
}
void Addition(int a, int b)
{
int Sum;
Sum = a + b;
printf("\n Addition of %d and %d is = %d \n", a, b, Sum);
}
```

```
Please Enter two integer values
Please enter two integer values
40
90
Addition of 40 and 90 is = 130
```

If you observe the main() function, We declared the integer variables a and b. This program allows the user to enter 2 integer values as a and b.

```
printf("\n Please Enter two integer values \n");
scanf("%d %d",&a, &b);
```

In the next line, we called the Addition (int a, int b) function with the user entered values

```
Addition(a, b);
```

Within the Addition (int a, int b) function,

We declared the integer variables of Sum, and also we have integer (a, b) arguments in the function. It means this function will allow the user to pass 2 integer values.

Next, we added both a and b using Arithmetic operator(+). In the next line, the printf statement is to print the output

```
printf("\n Addition of %d and %d is = %d \n", a, b, Sum);
```

4.34 C Function with argument and Return value

This method allows us to pass the arguments to the function while calling the function. This type of function will return some value when we call the function from main () or any sub function. Data Type of the return value will depend upon the return type of function declaration. For instance, if the return type is int then return value will be int.

This type of user-defined function is called a fully dynamic function, and it provides maximum control to the end-user.

Function with arguments and Return value Example

This Types of Functions in C program allows the user to enter 2 integer values. And then, we are going to pass those values to the user-defined function to multiply those values and return the value using the return keyword.

```
#include<stdio.h>
int Multiplication(int, int);
int main()
{
int a, b, Multi;
printf("\n Please Enter two integer values \n");
scanf("%d %d",&a, &b);
//Calling the function with dynamic values
Multi = Multiplication(a, b);
printf("\n Multiplication of %d and %d is = %d \n", a, b, Multi);
return 0;
}
int Multiplication(int a, int b)
{
int Multi;
Multi = a * b;
return Multi;
}
```

If you observe the main() function, we declared the integer variables Multi, a, and b. This program allows the user to enter 2 integer values as a and b.

```
printf("\n Please Enter two integer values \n");
scanf("%d %d",&a, &b);
```

In the next line, we assigned the return value of the Multiplication(int a, int b) function to the Multi integer. It is because the user-defined function also returns integer value only.

```
Multi = Multiplication(a, b);
```

We passed the user inputs as the arguments /parameters to the function Multiplication(int a, int b). In the next line, the printf statement prints the output

```
printf("\n Multiplication of a and b is = %d \n", Multi);
```

Within the Multiplication () function, we declared the integer variables of Multi, and also we have two integers (a, b) arguments in the function. It means this function will allow the user to pass two integer values. In the next line, we Multiplied both a and b using Arithmetic operator(*)

4.4 Parameter passing mechanism:

There are different ways in which parameter data can be passed into and out of methods and functions. Let us assume that a function *B()* is called from another function*A()*. In this case *A* is called the **"caller function"** and *B* is called the **"called function or callee function"**. Also, the arguments which *A* sends to *B* are called *actual arguments* and the parameters of *B* are called *formal arguments.*

Terminology

- **Formal Parameter: A** variable and its type as they appear in the prototype of the function or method.

- **Actual Parameter: The** variable or expression corresponding to a formal parameter that appears in the function or method call in the calling environment.

- **Modes:**

  - **IN:** Passes info from caller to calle.
  - **OUT:**Callee writes values in caller.
  - **IN/OUT:**Caller tells callee value of variable, which may be updated by caller.

  - **Important methods of Parameter Passing**

1. **Pass byValue: This** method uses *in-mode* semantics. Changes made to formal parameter do not get transmitted back to the caller. Any modifications to the formal parameter variable inside the called function or method affect only the separate storage location and will not be reflected in the actual parameter in the calling environment. This method is also called as*call by value.*

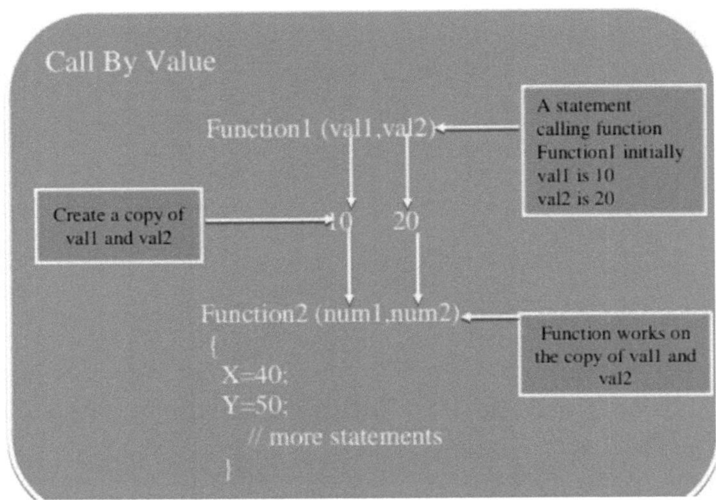


```
Example:
// C program to illustrate
// call by value
#include <stdio.h>
void func(int a, int b)
{
a += b;
printf("In func, a = %d b = %d\n", a, b);
}
int main(void)
{
int x = 5, y = 7;
// Passing parameters
func(x, y);
printf("In main, x = %d y = %d\n", x, y);
return 0;
```

```
}
```

Output:
In func, a = 12 b = 7
In main, x = 5 y = 7

2. Pass by reference (aliasing): This technique uses *in/out-mode* semantics. Changes made to formal parameter do get transmitted back to the caller through parameter passing. Any changes to the formal parameter are reflected in the actual parameter in the calling environment as formal parameter receives a reference (or pointer) to the actual data. This method is also called as **call by reference**. This method is efficient in both time and space.

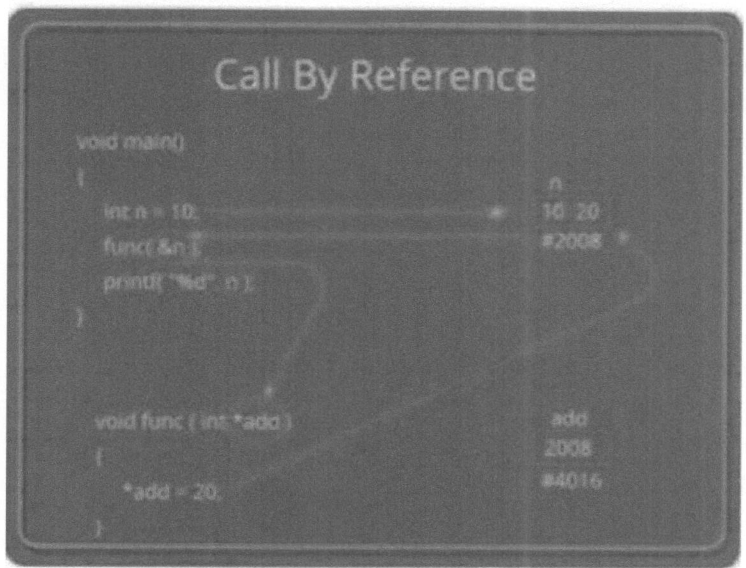

Example:

```
// C program to illustrate
// call by reference
#include <stdio.h>
void swapnum(int* i, int* j)
{
int temp = *i;
*i = *j;
*j = temp;
}
int main(void)
{
int a = 10, b = 20;
// passing parameters
swapnum(&a, &b);
printf("a is %d and b is %d\n", a, b);
return 0;
}
```

Output:
a is 20 and b is 10

4.5 Recursion in C

Recursion is the process which comes into existence when a function calls a copy of itself to work on a smaller problem. Any function which calls itself is called recursive function, and such function calls are called recursive calls. Recursion involves several numbers of recursive calls. However, it is important to impose a termination condition of recursion.

Recursion cannot be applied to all the problems, but it is more useful for the tasks that can be defined in terms of similar subtasks. For Example, recursion may be applied to sorting, searching, and traversal problems.

Generally, iterative solutions are more efficient than recursion since function call is always overhead. Any problem that can be solved recursively, can also be solved iteratively. However, some problems are best suited to be solved by the recursion, for example, tower of Hanoi, Fibonacci series, factorial finding, etc.

In the following example, recursion is used to calculate the factorial of a number.

```
#include <stdio.h>
int fact(int);
int main()
{
int n,f;
printf("Enter the number whose factorial you want to calculate?");
scanf("%d",&n);
f=fact(n);
printf("factorial=%d",f);
}
int fact(int n)
{
if(n==0)
{
return 0;
}
else if(n==1)
{
return 1;
}
else
{
return n*fact(n-1);
}
}
```

Output:

Enter the number whose factorial you want to calculate? 5

Factorial=120

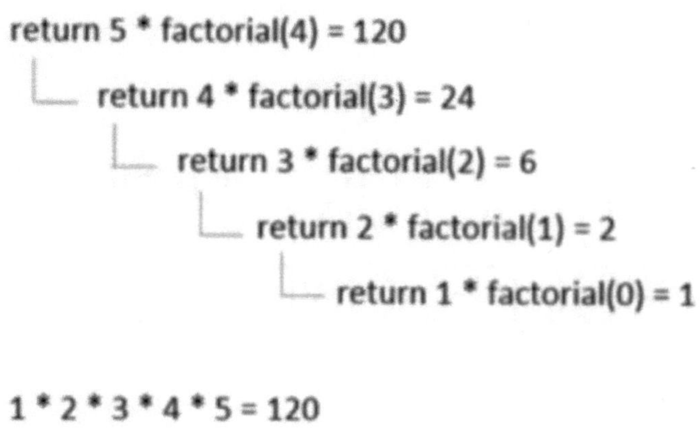

```
return 5 * factorial(4) = 120
└── return 4 * factorial(3) = 24
    └── return 3 * factorial(2) = 6
        └── return 2 * factorial(1) = 2
            └── return 1 * factorial(0) = 1

1 * 2 * 3 * 4 * 5 = 120
```

Fig: Recursion

4.6 Fibonacci Series:

Fibonacci Series: In case of Fibonacci series, *next number is the sum of previous two numbers* for example 0, 1, 1, 2, 3, 5, 8, 13, 21 etc. The first two numbers of Fibonacci series are 0 and 1.

Fibonacci Series using recursion in C

Let's see the Fibonacci series program in c using recursion.

```
#include<stdio.h>
void static int n1=0,n2=1,n3;
if(n>0){
n3=n1+n2;
n1=n2;
n2=n3;
printf("%d",n3);
printFibonacci(n-1);
}
}
int main(){
int n;
printf("Enter the number of elements:");
scanf("%d",&n);
printf("Fibonacci Series:");
printf("%d %d",0,1);
printFibonacci(n-2); //n-2 because 2 numbers are already printed
return 0;
}
```

Output:

```
Enter the number of elements:15
0 1 1 2 3 5 8 13 21 34 55 89 144 233 377
```

CHAPTER FIVE

Module-5 STRUCTURE ,POINTERS&PRE-PROCESSORDIRECTIVE

5.1 Structure:

Structure can be defined as collection of elements of different data types.

'struct' keyword is used to create a structure. **Following is an example.**

```
struct address
{
char name[50];
char street[100];
char city[50];
char state[20];
int pin;
};
```

A structure variable can either be declared with structure declaration or as a separate declaration like basic types.

```
// A variable declaration with structure declaration.
struct Point
{
int x, y;
} p1; // The variable p1 is declared with 'Point'
// A variable declaration like basic data types
struct Point
{
int x, y;
};
int main()
{
struct Point p1; // The variable p1 is declared like a normal variable
}
```

Structure members are accessed using dot (.) operator

```
#include<stdio.h>
struct Point
{
int x, y;
};
int main()
{
struct Point p1 ;
```

```
// accessing members of point p1
p1.x = 20;
p1.y=1;
printf ("x = %d, y = %d", p1.x, p1.y);
return 0;
}
```

Output:

x = 20, y = 1

5.11Array of structure:

Why use an array of structures?

Consider a case, where we need to store the data of 5 students. We can store it by using the structure as given below.

```
#include<stdio.h>
struct student
{
char name[20];
int id;
float marks;
};
void main()
{
struct student s1,s2,s3;
int dummy;
printf("Enter the name, id, and marks of student 1 ");
scanf("%s%d%f",s1.name,&s1.id,&s1.marks);
printf("Enter the name, id, and marks of student 2 ");
scanf("%s%d%f",s2.name,&s2.id,&s2.marks);
printf("Enter the name, id, and marks of student 3 ");
scanf("%s%d%f",s3.name,&s3.id,&s3.marks);
printf("Printing the details....\n");
printf("%s%d %f\n",s1.name,s1.id,s1.marks);
printf("%s%d%f\n",s2.name,s2.id,s2.marks);
printf("%s %d %f\n",s3.name,s3.id,s3.marks);
}
```

Output:

Enter the name, id, and marks of student 1 James 90 90

```
Enter the name, id, and marks of student 2 Adoms 90 90
Enter the name, id, and marks of student 3 Nick 90 90
Printing the details....
James 90 90.000000
Adoms 90 90.000000
Nick 90 90.000000
```

In the above program, we have stored data of 3 students in the structure. However, the complexity of the program will be increased if there are 20 students. In that case, we will have to declare 20 different structure variables and store them one by one. This will always be tough since we will have to declare a variable every time we add a student. Remembering the name of all the variables is also a very tricky task. However, c enables us to declare an array of structures by using which, we can avoid declaring the different structure variables; instead

we can make a collection containing all the structures that store the information of different entities.

5.11 Array of Structures in C

An array of structures in C can be defined as the collection of multiple structures variables where each variable contains information about different entities. The array of structures in Cis used to store information about multiple entities of different data types. The array of structures is also known as the collection of structures.

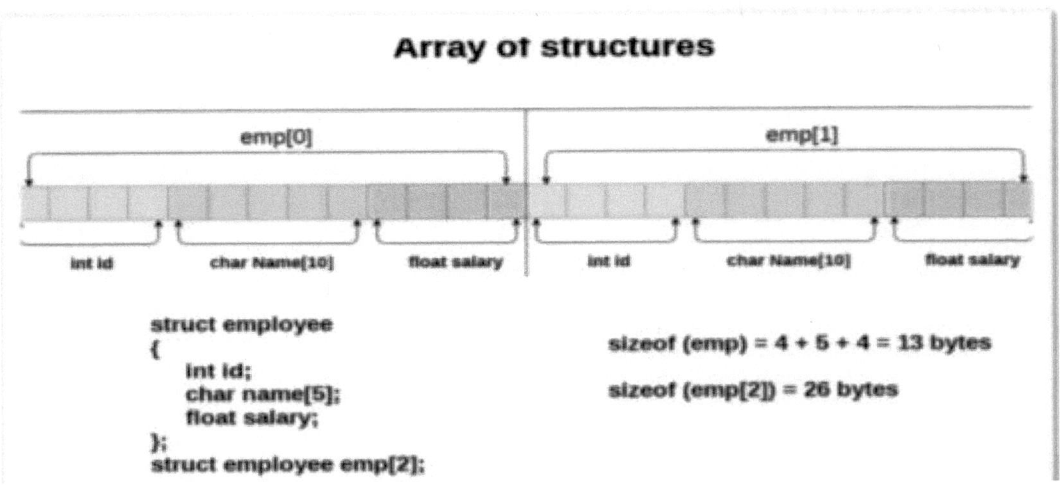

Fig 5.11: Array of structures

et's see an example of an array of structures that stores information of 5 students and prints it.

```
#include<stdio.h>
#include<string.h>
struct student{
int rollno;
char name[10];
};
int main(){
int i;
struct student st[5];
printf("Enter Records of 5 students");
for(i=0;i<5;i++){
printf("\nEnter Rollno:");
scanf("%d",&st[i].rollno);
printf("\nEnter Name:");
scanf("%s",&st[i].name);
}
printf("\nStudent Information List:");
for(i=0;i<5;i++){
printf("\nRollno:%d, Name:%s",st[i].rollno,st[i].name);
}
return 0;
```

```
}
```

Output:

```
Enter Records of 5 students
Enter Rollno:1
Enter Name:Sonoo
Enter Rollno:2
Enter Name:Ratan
Enter Rollno:3
Enter Name:Vimal
Enter Rollno:4
Enter Name:James
Enter Rollno:5
Enter Name:Sarfraz
Student Information List:
Rollno:1, Name:Sonoo
Rollno:2, Name:Ratan
Rollno:3, Name:Vimal
Rollno:4, Name:James
Rollno:5, Name:Sarfraz
```

5.12 Nested structure:

C provides us the feature of nesting one structure within another structure by using which, complex data types are created. For example, we may need to store the address of an entity employee in a structure. The attribute address may also have the subparts as street number, city, state, and pin code. Hence, to store the address of the employee, we need to store the address of the employee into a separate structure and nest the structure address into the structure employee. Consider the following program.

```
#include<stdio.h>
struct address
{
char city[20];
int pin;
char phone[14];
};
struct employee
{
char name[20];
struct address add;
};
void main ()
{
struct employee emp;
printf("Enter employee information?\n");
scanf("%s%s%d%s",emp.name,emp.add.city,&emp.add.pin,emp.add.phone);
printf("Printing the employee information....\n");
printf("name:%s\nCity:%s\nPincode:%d\nPhone:%s",emp.name,emp.add.city,emp.add.pin,emp.add.phone);
}
```

Output:

Enter employee information?

```
Arun
```

```
Delhi
110001
1234567890
Printing the employee information....
name: Arun
City: Delhi
Pincode: 110001
Phone: 1234567890
```

5.13 Structures & functions:

Passing structs to functions

Here's how you can pass structures to a function

```
#include <stdio.h>
struct student {
char name[50];
int age;
};
// function prototype
void display(struct student s);
int main() {
struct student s1;
printf("Enter name: ");
// read string input from the user until \n is entered
// \n is discarded
scanf("%c", s1.name);
printf("Enter age: ");
scanf("%d", &s1.age);
display(s1); // passing struct as an argument
return 0;
}
void display(struct student s) {
printf("\nDisplaying information\n");
printf("Name: %s", s.name);
printf("\nAge: %d", s.age);
}
```

Output:

```
Enter name: Smith
Enter age: 13
Displaying information
Name: Smith
Age: 13
```

5.14 Passing struct by reference:

You can also pass structs by reference (in a similar way like you pass variables of built-in type by reference). During pass by reference, the memory addresses of struct variables are passed to the function

```
#include <stdio.h>
```

```
typedef struct Complex
{
float real;
float imag;
} complex;
void addNumbers(complex c1, complex c2, complex *result);
int main()
{
complex c1, c2, result;
printf("For first number,\n");
printf("Enter real part: ");
scanf("%f", &c1.real);
printf("Enter imaginary part: ");
scanf("%f", &c1.imag);
printf("For second number, \n");
printf("Enter real part: ");
scanf("%f", &c2.real);
printf("Enter imaginary part: ");
scanf("%f", &c2.imag);
addNumbers(c1, c2, &result);
printf("\nresult.real = %.1f\n", result.real);
printf("result.imag = %.1f", result.imag);
return 0;
}
void addNumbers(complex c1, complex c2, complex *result)
{
result->real = c1.real + c2.real;
result->imag = c1.imag + c2.imag;
}
```

Output:

```
For first number,
Enter real part: 1.1
Enter imaginary part: -2.4
For second number,
Enter real part: 3.4
Enter imaginary part: -3.2
result.real = 4.5
result.imag = -5.6
```

5.15 typedef in C:

The typedef is a keyword used in C programming to provide some meaningful names to the already existing variable in the C program. It behaves similarly as we define the alias for the commands. In short, we can say that this keyword is used to redefine the name of an already existing variable.

Syntax of typedef

Typedef <existing_name><alias_name>

n the above syntax, 'existing_name' is the name of an already existing variable while 'alias name' is another name given to the existing variable.

For example, suppose we want to create a variable of type unsigned int, then it becomes a tedious task if we want to declare multiple variables of this type. To overcome the problem, we use a typedef keyword.

typedef unsigned int unit;

In the above statements, we have declared the unit variable of type unsigned int by using a typedef keyword.

Now, we can create the variables of type unsigned int by writing the following statement:

unit a, b;

instead of writing:

unsigned int a, b;

ill now, we have observed that the typedef keyword provides a nice shortcut by providing an alternative name for an already existing variable. This keyword is useful when we are dealing with the long data type especially, structure declarations.

Let's understand through a simple example.

```
#include<stdio.h>
int main()
{
typedef unsigned int unit;
unit i,j;
i=10;
j=20;
printf("Value of i is :%d",i);
printf("\nValue of j is:%d",j);
return 0;
}
```

Output

```
Value of i is :10
Value of j is :20
```

Using typedef with structures

Consider the below structure declaration:

```
struct student
{
char name[20];
int age;
};
struct student s1;
```

In the above structure declaration, we have created the variable of student type by writing the following statement:

struct student s1;

The above statement shows the creation of a variable, i.e., s1, but the statement is quite big. To avoid such a big statement, we use the typedef keyword to create the variable of type student.

```
Struct student
{
char name[20];
int age;
};
```

```
typedef struct student stud;
stud s1,s2;
```

In the above statement, we have declared the variable stud of type struct student. Now, we can use the stud variable in a program to create the variables of type struct student.

The above typedef can be written as:

```
typedef struct student
{
char name[20];
int age;
}stud;
stud s1,s2;
```

From the above declarations, we conclude that typedef keyword reduces the length of the code and complexity of data types. It also helps in understanding the program.

5.16 Pointers & functions:

Pointers give great possibilities to 'C' functions which we are limited to return one value. With pointer parameters, our functions now can process actual data rather than a copy of data.

In order to modify the actual values of variables, the calling statement passes addresses to pointer parameters in a function.

Functions Pointers Example

For example, the next program swaps two values of two:

```
void swap (int *a, int *b);
int main() {
int m = 25;
int n = 100;
printf("m is %d, n is %d\n", m, n);
swap(&m, &n);
printf("m is %d, n is %d\n", m, n);
return 0;}
void swap (int *a, int *b) {
int temp;
temp = *a;
*a = *b;
*b = temp;}
}
```

Output:

```
m is 25, n is 100
m is 100, n is 25
```

```
void swap (int *a, int *b);
int main() {
  int m = 25;
  int n = 100;
  printf("m is %d, n is %d\n", m, n);
  swap(&m, &n);
  printf("m is %d, n is %d\n", m, n);
  return 0;}
void swap (int *a, int *b) {
  int temp;
  temp = *a;
  *a = *b;
  *b = temp;}
```

The program swaps the actual variables values because the function accesses them by address using pointers. Here we will discuss the program process:

- We declare the function responsible for swapping the two variable values, which takes two integer pointers as parameters and returns any value when it is called.
- In the main function, we declare and initialize two integer variables ('m' and 'n') then we print their values respectively.
- We call the swap() function by passing the address of the two variables as arguments using the ampersand symbol. After that, we print the new swapped values of variables.
- Here we define the swap() function content which takes two integer variable addresses as parameters and declare a temporary integer variable used as a third storage box to save one of the value variables which will be put to the second variable.
- Save the content of the first variable pointed by 'a' in the temporary variable.
- Store the second variable pointed by b in the first variable pointed by a.
- Update the second variable (pointed by b) by the value of the first variable saved in the temporary variable.

Functions with Array Parameters

In C, we cannot pass an array by value to a function. Whereas, an array name is a pointer (address), so we just pass an array name to a function which means to pass a pointer to the array.

For example, we consider the following program:

```
int add_array (int *a, int num_elements);
int main() {
int Tab[5] = {100, 220, 37, 16, 98};
printf("Total summation is %d\n", add_array(Tab, 5));
return 0;}
int add_array (int *p, int size) {
int total = 0;
```

```
int k;
for (k = 0; k < size; k++) {
total += p[k]; /* it is equivalent to total +=*p ;p++; */}
return (total);}
```

Output:

Total summation is 471

Here, we will explain the program code with its details

```
int add_array (int *a, int num_elements);
int main() {
  int Tab[5] = {100, 220, 37, 16, 98};
  printf("Total summation is %d\n", add_array(Tab, 5));
  return 0;}
int add_array (int *p, int size) {
  int total = 0;
  int k;
  for (k = 0; k < size; k++) {
    total += p[k];
 return (total);}
```

- We declare and define add_array() function which takes an array address(pointer) with its elements number as parameters and returns the total accumulated summation of these elements. The pointer is used to iterate the array elements (using the p[k] notation), and we accumulate the summation in a local variable which will be returned after iterating the entire element array.
- We declare and initialize an integer array with five integer elements. We print the total summation by passing the array name (which acts as address) and array size to the add_array()called function as arguments.

5.2 Pointers:

Pointers store address of variables or a memory location rather than values.

Address in C

If you have a variable var in your program,&var will give you its address in the memory.

We have used address numerous times while using scanf() function.

```
scanf("%d", &var);
```

Here, the value entered by the user is stored in the address of var variable. Let's take a working example.

```
#include <stdio.h>
int main()
{
int var = 5;
printf("var: %d\n", var);
// Notice the use of & before var
printf("address of var: %p", &var);
return 0;
}
```

Output

var: 5
address of var: 2686778

Pointer Syntax

Here is how we can declare pointers.

```
int* p;
```

Here, we have declared a pointer p of int type.

You can also declare pointers in these ways.

```
int *p1;
int * p2;
```

Let's take another example of declaring pointers.

```
int* p1, p2;
```

Here, we have declared a pointer p1 and a normal variable p2.

Assigning addresses to Pointers

Let's take an example.

```
int* pc, c;
c = 5;
pc = &c;
```

Here, 5 is assigned to the c variable. And, the address of c is assigned to the pc pointer.

Get Value of variable Pointed by Pointers

To get the value of the thing pointed by the pointers, we use the * operator. For example:

```
int* pc, c;
c = 5;
pc = &c;
printf("%d", *pc); // Output: 5
```

Here, the address of c is assigned to the pc pointer. To get the value stored in that address, we used *pc.

Changing Value Pointed by Pointers

Let's take an example.

```
int* pc, c;
c = 5;
pc = &c;
c = 1;
printf("%d", c); // Output: 1
printf("%d", *pc); // Output: 1
```

We have assigned the address of c to the pc pointer.

Then, we changed the value of c to 1. Since pc and the address of c is the same,*pc gives us 1.

Let's take another example.

```
int* pc, c;
c = 5;
pc = &c;
*pc = 1;
printf("%d", *pc); // Output: 1
printf("%d", c); // Output: 1
```

We have assigned the address of c to the pc pointer.

Then, we changed *pc to 1 using *pc=1;. Since pc and the address of c is the same, c will be equal to 1.

Let's take one more example.

```
int* pc, c, d;
c = 5;
d = -15;
pc = &c; printf("%d", *pc); // Output: 5
pc = &d; printf("%d", *pc); // Output: -15
```

Initially, the address of c is assigned to the pc pointer usingpc=&c;. Since c is 5,*pcgives us 5.

Then, the address of d is assigned to the pc pointer using pc=&d;. Since d is -15, *pcgives us -15.

Example: Working of Pointers

Let's take a working example.

```
#include <stdio.h>
int main()
{
int* pc, c;
c = 22;
printf("Address of c: %p\n", &c);
printf("Value of c: %d\n\n", c); // 22
pc = &c;
printf("Address of pointer pc: %p\n", pc);
printf("Content of pointer pc: %d\n\n", *pc); // 22
c = 11;
printf("Address of pointer pc: %p\n", pc);
printf("Content of pointer pc: %d\n\n", *pc); // 11
*pc = 2;
printf("Address of c: %p\n", &c);
printf("Value of c: %d\n\n", c); // 2
return 0;
}
```

Output

```
Address of c: 2686784
Value of c: 22
Address of pointer pc: 2686784
Content of pointer pc: 22
Address of pointer pc: 2686784
Content of pointer pc: 11
Address of c: 2686784
Value of c: 2
```

Explanation of the program

1.int* pc, c;

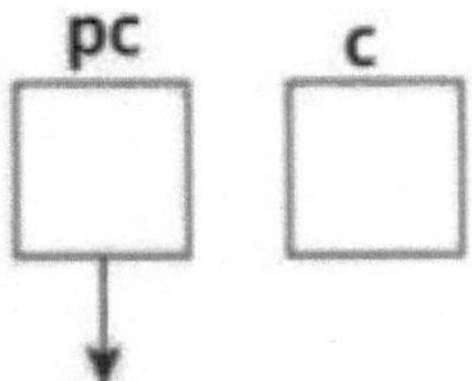

Here, a pointer pc and a normal variable c, both of type int, is created.

Since pc and c are not initialized at initially, pointer pc points to either no address or a random address. And, variable c has an address but contains random garbage

2.c = 22;

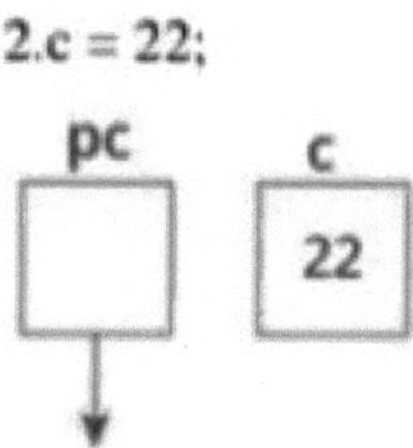

This assigns 22 to the variable c. That is, 22 is stored in the memory location of variable c.

3.pc = &c;

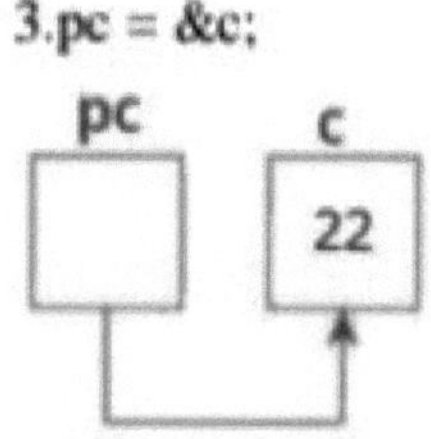

This assigns the address of variable c to the pointer pc.

4.c = 11;

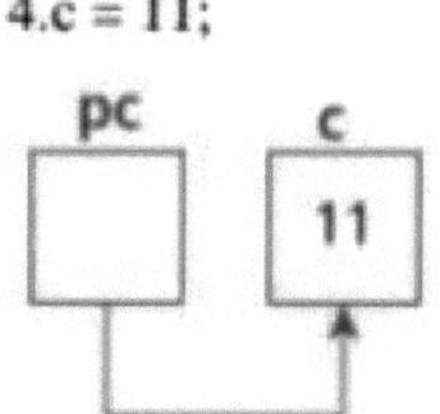

This assigns 11 to variable c.

5.*pc = 2;

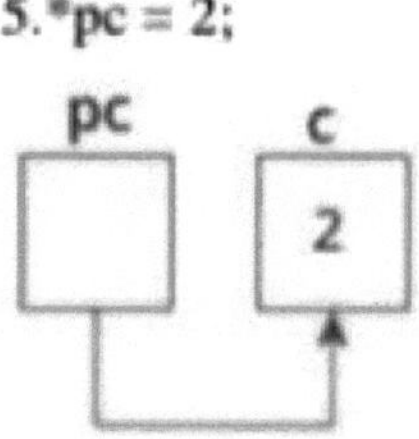

This change the value at the memory location pointed by the pointer pc to 2.

This change the value at the memory location pointed by the pointer pc to 2.

Advantages & disadvantages of pointers:

Advantages:

- Pointers provide direct access to memory.
- Pointers provide a way to return more than one value to the functions.
- Reduces the storage space and complexity of the program.
- Reduces the execution time of the program.

- Provides an alternate way to access array elements.
- Pointers can be used to pass information back and forth between the calling function and called function.
- Pointers allows us to perform dynamic memory allocation and deallocation.
- Pointers helps us to build complex data structures like linked list, stack, queues, trees, graphs etc.
- Pointers allow us to resize the dynamically allocated memory block.
- Addresses of objects can be extracted using pointers.

Disadvantages:

- Uninitialized pointers might cause segmentation fault.
- Dynamically allocated block needs to be freed explicitly. Otherwise, it would lead to memory leak.
- Pointers are slower than normal variables.
- If pointers are updated with incorrect values, it might lead to memory corruption.

5.21 Dynamic Memory Allocation:

As you know, an array is a collection of a fixed number of values. Once the size of an array is declared, you cannot change it.

Sometimes the size of the array you declared may be insufficient. To solve this issue, you can allocate memory manually during run-time. This is known as dynamic memory allocation in C programming.

To allocate memory dynamically, library functions are malloc(),calloc(),realloc() and free() are used. These functions are defined in the <stdlib.h> header file.

malloc()

The name "malloc" stands for memory allocation.The malloc() function reserves a block of memory of the specified number of bytes. And, it returns a pointer of void() which can be casted into pointers of any form.

Syntax of malloc()

ptr = (castType*) malloc(size);

Example

ptr = (float*) malloc(100 * sizeof(float));

The above statement allocates 400 bytes of memory. It's because the size of float is 4 bytes. And, the pointer ptr holds the address of the first byte in the allocated memory.

The expression results in a NULL pointer if the memory cannot be allocated.

calloc()

The name "calloc" stands for contiguous allocation.

The malloc() function allocates memory and leaves the memory uninitialized, whereas the calloc() function allocates memory and initializes all bits to zero.

Syntax of calloc()

ptr = (castType*)calloc(n, size);

Example:

ptr = (float*) calloc(25, sizeof(float));

The above statement allocates contiguous space in memory for 25 elements of type float .

free()

Dynamically allocated memory created with either calloc() or malloc() doesn't get freed on their own. You must explicitly use free() to release the space.

Syntax of free()

free(ptr);

This statement frees the space allocated in the memory pointed by ptr.

Example 1: malloc() and free()

```
// Program to calculate the sum of n numbers entered by the user
#include <stdio.h>
#include <stdlib.h>
int main() {
int n, i, *ptr, sum = 0;
printf("Enter number of elements: ");
scanf("%d", &n);
ptr = (int*) malloc(n * sizeof(int));
// if memory cannot be allocated
if(ptr == NULL) {
printf("Error! memory not allocated.");
exit(0);
}
printf("Enter elements: ");
for(i = 0; i < n; ++i) {
scanf("%d", ptr + i);
sum += *(ptr + i);
}
printf("Sum = %d", sum);
// deallocating the memory
free(ptr);
return 0;
}
```

Output

```
Enter number of elements: 3
Enter elements: 100
20
36
Sum = 156
```

Here, we have dynamically allocated the memory for n number of int.

Example 2: calloc() and free()

```
// Program to calculate the sum of n numbers entered by the user
#include <stdio.h>
#include <stdlib.h>
int main() {
int n, i, *ptr, sum = 0;
printf("Enter number of elements: ");
scanf("%d", &n);
ptr = (int*) calloc(n, sizeof(int));
if(ptr == NULL) {
printf("Error! memory not allocated.");
exit(0);
}
printf("Enter elements: ");
for(i = 0; i < n; ++i) {
scanf("%d", ptr + i);
sum += *(ptr + i);
}
printf("Sum = %d", sum);
free(ptr);
return 0;
}
Output
Enter number of elements: 3
Enter elements: 100
20
36
Sum = 156
```

realloc()

If the dynamically allocated memory is insufficient or more than required, you can change the size of previously allocated memory using the realloc() function.

Syntax of realloc()

ptr = realloc(ptr, x);

Here, ptr is reallocated with a new size x.

Example 3: realloc()

```
#include <stdio.h>
#include <stdlib.h>
int main() {
int *ptr, i , n1, n2;
printf("Enter size: ");
scanf("%d", &n1);
ptr = (int*) malloc(n1 * sizeof(int));
printf("Addresses of previously allocated memory:\n");
```

```
for(i = 0; i < n1; ++i)
printf("%pc\n",ptr + i);
printf("\nEnter the new size: ");
scanf("%d", &n2);
// rellocating the memory
ptr = realloc(ptr, n2 * sizeof(int));
printf("Addresses of newly allocated memory:\n");
for(i = 0; i < n2; ++i)
printf("%pc\n", ptr + i);
free(ptr);
return 0;
}
```

Output

```
Enter size: 2
Addresses of previously allocated memory:
26855472
26855476
Enter the new size: 4
Addresses of newly allocated memory:
26855472
26855476
26855480
26855484
```

5.3 Pre-processor Directives:

The C pre-processor is a microprocessor that is used by compiler to transform your code before compilation. It is called micro pre-processor because it allows us to add macros.

A macro is a fragment of code that is given a name. You can define a macro in C using the #define preprocessor directive.

All pre-processor directives starts with hash # symbol.

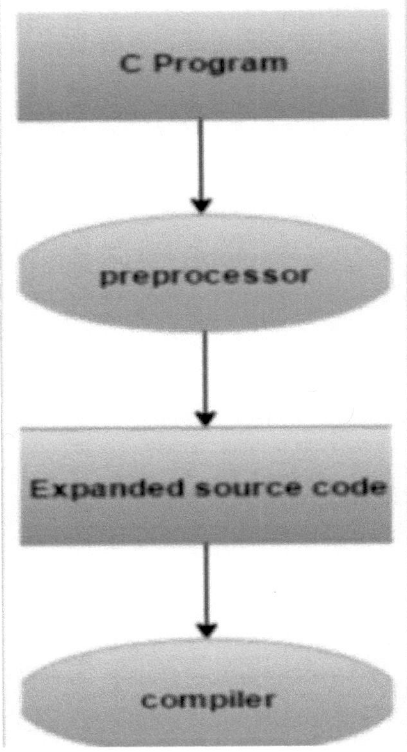

Fig 5.3:Pre-processor Directives

Let's see a list of pre-processor directives.

Sl No.	Directive & Description
1	#define Substitutes a pre-processor macro.
2	#include Inserts a particular header from another file.
3	#undef Undefines a pre-processor macro.
4	#ifdef Returns true if this macro is defined.
5	#ifndef Returns true if this macro is not defined.
6	#if Tests if a compile time condition is true.
7	#else The alternative for #if.
8	#elif #else and #if in one statement.
9	#endif Ends pre-processor conditional.
10	#error Prints error message on stderr.
11	#pragma Issues special commands to the compiler, using a standardized method.

Issues special commands to the compiler, using a standardized method.

5.31 C Predefined Macros

A macro is a segment of code which is replaced by the value of macro.ANSI C defines many predefined macros that can be used in c program.

No.	Macro	Description
1	_DATE_	Represents current date in "MMM DD YYYY" format.
2	_TIME_	Represents current time in "HH:MM:SS" format.
3	_FILE_	Represents current file name.
4	_LINE_	Represents current line number.
5	_STDC_	It is defined as 1 when compiler complies with the ANSI standard.

CHAPTER SIX

COMPUTER PROGRAMMING LABORATORY

COMPUTER PROGRAMMING LABORATORY

COMPUTER PROGRAMMING LABORATORY SEMESTER – I/II			
Laboratory Code	18CPL17/27	CIE Marks	40
Number of Lecture Hours/Week	0:0:2	SEE Marks	60
Total Number of Lab Contact Hours	30	Exam Hours	03
CREDITS – 01			

Laboratory Programs:

1. Familiarization with computer hardware and programming environment, concept of namingthe
2. Program files, storing, compilation, execution and debugging. Taking any simple C- code.

PART - A

1. Develop a program to solve simple computational problems using arithmetic expressions anduse of
2. Each operator leading to simulation of a commercial calculator. (No built-in mathfunction)
3. Develop a program to compute the roots of a quadratic equation by accepting thecoefficients.
4. Print appropriate messages.
5. Develop a program to find the reverse of a positive integer and check for palindrome or not.
6. Display appropriate messages.
7. An electricity board charges the following rates for the use of electricity: for the first 200 units 80
8. Paisa per unit: for the next 100 units 90 paisa per unit: beyond 300 units Rs 1 perunit. All users

   Are charged a minimum of Rs. 100 as meter charge. If the total amount is morethan Rs 400, then an additional surcharge of 15% of total amount is charged. Write a programto read the name of the user, number of units consumed and print out the charges.

11. Introduce 1D Array manipulation and implement Binary search.
12. Implement using functions to check whether the given number is prime and displayappropriate

messages. (No built-in math function)

PART - B

13. Develop a program to introduce 2D Array manipulation and implement Matrix multiplicationand ensure the rules of multiplication are checked.
14. Develop a Program to compute Sin(x) using Taylor series approximation. Compare yourresult with the built- in Library function. Print both the results with appropriate messages.
15. Write functions to implement string operations such as compare, concatenate, string length.Convince The parameter passing techniques.
16. Develop a program to sort the given set of N numbers using Bubble sort.
17. Develop a program to find the square root of a given number N and execute for all possibleinputs With appropriate messages. Note: Don't use library function sqrt(n).
18. Implement structures to read, write, and compute average- marks and the students scoring above and below the average marks for a class of N students.
19. Develop a program using pointers to compute the sum, mean and standard deviation of allelements stored in an array of n real numbers.
20. Implement Recursive functions for Binary to Decimal Conversion.

Program 2: Develop a program to solve simple computational problems using arithmetic expressions anduse of each operator leading to simulation of a commercial calculator. (No built-in mathfunction).

```
#include<stdio.h>
#include<stdlib.h>
void main()
{
int ch,a,b;
float res;
printf("Enter two numbers:\n");
scanf("%d%d",&a,&b);
printf("1=Add, 2=Sub, 3=Mul, 4=Div, 5=Rem\n"); printf("Enter your choice:\n"); scanf("%d",&ch);
switch(ch)
{case 1: res=a+b;
break;
                                                            case 2: res=a-b;
                                                                  break;
                                                            case 3: res=a*b;
break;
```

```
case 4: res=(float)a/b;
break;
case 5: res=a%b;
break;
default: printf("Entered Wrong choice\n");
}
printf("Result=%d\n",res);
}
```

Output

```
Enter two numbers: 10
20
1=Add, 2=Sub, 3=Mul, 4=Div, 5=Rem
Enter your choice:1
Result=30
```

Program 3: Develop a program to compute the roots of a quadratic equation by accepting thecoefficients. Print appropriate messages.

```
#include<stdio.h>
#include<stdlib.h>
#include<math.h>
int main( )
{
float a, b, c, root1, root2, rpart, ipart, disc;
printf("Enter the 3 coefficients:\n");
scanf(%f%f%f", &a, &b, &c);
if((a*b*c) = = 0)
{
printf("Roots cannot be Determined:\n");
exit(0);
}
disc = (b*b) - (4*a*c);
if(disc = = 0)
{
printf("Roots are equal\n");
root1=root2= -b / (2*a);
printf("root1=root2=%f",root1);
}
else if(disc>0)
{
printf("Roots are real and distinct\n");
root1= (-b + sqrt(disc)) / (2*a);
root2= (-b - sqrt(disc)) / (2*a);
printf ("root1 = %f \n root2 = %f\n", root1, root2);
}
else
{printf("Roots are complex\n");
rpart = -b / (2*a);
ipart = (sqrt (-disc)) / (2*a);
printf("root1 = %f + i %f \n", rpart, ipart);
```

```
printf("root2 = %f - i %f \n", rpart, ipart);
}
}
```

Output

First Run:

Enter the 3 coefficients:
1
2
1
Roots are equal
root1=root2=-1.000000

Second Run:

Enter the 3 coefficients:
2
3
2
Roots are real and equal
root1=-0.500000
root2=-2.000000

Third Run:

Enter the 3 coefficients:
2
2
2
Roots are complex
root1=-0.500000+i 0.866025
root2=-0.500000- i 0.866025

Viva Questions:

a. What is quadratic Equation?

b. What is math.h ? why it is used in C program?

c. What are decision making statements in C language?

d. Write the syntax of " if "statement?

Difference between if and switch statements?

Program 4: Develop a program to find the reverse of a positive integer and check for palindrome or not.Display appropriate messages.

```
#include<stdio.h>
int main()
{
int digitno, num, rev, rem;
printf("Enter the integer number:\n");
scanf ("%d", &digitno);
num = digitno;
rev=0;
```

```
printf("The given integer number = %d\n",num);
while(digitno != 0)
{
rem = digitno % 10;
rev = rev * 10 + rem;
digitno = digitno / 10;
}
printf("The reversed number is %d\n", rev);
if(num = = rev)
printf("The given number %d is a palindrome\n", num); else
                                    printf("The given number %d is not a palindrome\n", num);
}
```

Output:

First Run:

Enter the integer number
2442
The given integer number = 2442
The reversed number 2442
The given number 2442 is a palindrome

Second Run:

Enter the integer number
1234
The given integer number = 1234
The reversed number 4321
The given number 1234 is not a palindrome

Program 5: An electricity board charges the following rates for the use of electricity: for the first 200 units 80 paise per unit: for the next 100 units 90 paise per unit: beyond 300 units Rs 1 perunit. All users are charged a minimum of Rs. 100 as meter charge. If the total amount is morethan Rs 400, then an additional surcharge of 15% of total amount is charged. Write a programto read the name of the user, number of units consumed and print out the charges.

```
#include <stdio.h>
void main()
{
char name[10];
float unit, amt;
printf("Enter your name and unit Consumed:");
scanf("%s %f",name,&unit);
if(unit<=200)
amt=unit*0.80+100;
else if((unit>200)&&(unit<=300))
amt=200*0.80+((unit-200)*0.90)+100;
else
amt=200*0.80+100*0.90+((unit-300)*1)+100;
if(amt>400)
amt=1.15*amt;
                                    printf("Name: %s\n Unit=%f \n charge=%f ",name,unit,amt);
}
```

Output

First Run

Enter your name and unit Consumed: Siri 52
Name: Siri
Unit=52
charge=141.600000

Second Run

Enter your name and unit Consumed: Rajesh
460

Name: Rajesh
Unit=460
charge=586.500000

Program 6: Introduce 1D Array manipulation and implement Binary search.

```
#include<stdio.h>
void main()
{
int n, a[100], i, key, high, low, mid, loc=-1;
printf("Enter the size of the array\n");
scanf("%d",&n);
printf("Enter the elements of array in sorted order\n");
for(i=0;i<n;i++)
scanf("%d",&a[i]);
printf("Enter the key element to be searched\n");
scanf("%d",&key);
low=0;
high=n-1;
while(low<=high)
{
mid=(low+high)/2;
if(key==a[mid])
{
loc = mid+1;
break;
}
else
{
if(key<a[mid])
high=mid-1;
else
low=mid+1;
}
}
if(loc>0)
printf("\n The element %d is found at %d ",key,loc);
else
printf("\nThe search is unsuccessful");
}
```

Output

First Run

Enter the size of the array

5
Enter the elements of array in sorted order
10
20
30
40
50
Enter the element to be searched
40
The element 40 is found at 4

Program 7: Implement using functions to check whether the given number is prime and displayappropriate messages. (No built-in math function)

```
#include<stdio.h>
int isprime(int);
int main()
{
int num;
printf("Enter value of num:\n");
scanf("%d",&num);
if (isprime(num))
printf("%d is a prime number",num);
else
Printf("%d is not a prime number",num)
}
int isprime(int x)
{
int i;
for(i=2;i<=x/2;i++)
if(x%i == 0)
return 0;
return 1;
}
```

Output:

Run1

Enter value of num:
17
17 is a prime number

Run1

Enter value of num:
10
10 is not a prime number

Program 8: Develop a program to introduce 2D Array manipulation and implement Matrix multiplicationand ensure the rules of multiplication are checked.

```
#include<stdio.h>
#include<stdlib.h>
int main( )
{
int m,n,p,q,row,col,k,a[3][3],b[3][3],c[3][3];
```

```
printf("Enter the order of matrix A\n");
scanf("%d%d",&m,&n);
printf("enter order of matrix B\n");
scanf("%d%d",&p,&q);
if(n!=p)
{
printf("Matrix Multiplication is not possible\n"); exit(0);
}
printf("Enter the elements into matrix A\n");
for(row=0;row<m;row++)
{
for(col=0;col<n;col++)
{
scanf("%d",&a[row][col]);
}
}
printf("Enter the elements into matrix B\n");
for(row=0;row<p;row++)
{
for(col=0;col<q ;col++)
{
scanf("%d",&b[row][col]);
}
}
for(row=0;row<m;row++)
{
for(col=0;col<q;col++)
{
c[row][col]=0;
for(k=0;k<n;k++)
{
                                                  c[row][col]= c[row][col]+a[row][k]*b[k][col];
}
}
}
printf("The elements of matrix A are\n");
for(row=0;row<m;row++)
{
for(col=0;col<n;col++)
{
printf("%3d",a[row][col]);
}
printf("\n");
}
printf("The elements of matrix B are\n");
for(row=0;row<p;row++)
{
for(col=0;col<q;col++)
```

```
{
printf("%3d",b[row][col]);
}
printf("\n");
}
printf("Product of Matrix A and B is\n");
for(row=0;row<m;row++)
{
for(col=0;col<q;col++)
{
printf("%3d",c[row][col]);
}
printf("\n");
}}
```

Output:

Enter the order of matrix A

2 2

Enter the order of matrix B

2 2

Enter the elements into matrix A

1 2 3 4

Enter the elements into matrix B

5 6 7 8

Elements of matrix A are

1. **2**

3. **4**

Elements of matrix B are

5. **6**

7. **8**

Product of matrix A and B is

19. **22**

43. **50**

Program 9: Develop a Program to compute Sin(x) using Taylor series approximation. Compare yourresult with the built- in Library function. Print both the results with appropriate messages.

```
#include<stdio.h>
#include<math.h>
int main( )
{
int i;
```

```
float x,t,sum,sum1,y;
printf("Enter the angle\n");
scanf("%f",&x);
y=x;
x=3.1428*(x/180.0);
sum=x;
t=x;
i=1;
do
{
i=i+2;
t=(-t*x*x)/((i-1)*i);
sum=sum+t;
}while(fabs(t)>0.00005);
printf("sin(%f) using taylor series=%f\n",y,sum); sum1=sin(x);
printf("Using inbuilt function sin(%f)=%f",y,sum1); }
```

Output:

Enter the angle 30

sin(30.000000) using taylor series=0.500000

Using inbuilt function sin(30.000000)=0.500000

Program 10: Write functions to implement string operations such as compare, concatenate, string length.Convince the parameter passing techniques.

```
#include<stdio.h>
#include<string.h>
void compare(char [ ],char [ ]);
void concat(char [ ],char [ ]);
void length(char *[ ]);
void main( )
{
int n,digit;
char str1[10],str2[10];
do
{
printf("press 1-compare 2-concatenate 3-length of string"); printf("\n enter your choice="); scanf("%d",&n);
switch(n)
{
case 1:printf("enter first string=");
scanf("%s",str1);
printf("enter second string=");
scanf("%s",str2);
compare(str1,str2);
break;
case 2: printf("enter first string=");
scanf("%s",str1);
printf("enter second string=");
scanf("%s",str2);
concat(str1,str2);
break;
```

```
case 3:printf("enter string=");
scanf("%s",str1);
length(&str1);
break;
default: printf("wrong choice");
break;
}
printf("\n Do you want to continue(1/0)? ");
scanf("%d", &digit);
}while(digit==1);
}
void compare(char str1[ ],char str2[ ])
{
int i;
i=strcmp(str1,str2);
if(i==0)
printf("strings are equal\n ");
else
printf("string are not equal\n");
}
void concat(char str1[ ],char str2[ ])
{
strcat(str1,str2);
printf("concatenate string=%s",str1);
}
void length(char *str1[ ])
{
int len;
len=strlen(str1);
printf("the length of string=%d",len);
}
```

Output

press 1-compare 2-concatenate 3-length of string
enter your choice=1
enter first string=ram
enter second string=Ram
string are not equal
Do you want to continue(1/0)? 1
press 1-compare 2-concatenate 3-length of string
enter your choice=2
enter first string=RAM
enter second string=kumar
concatenate string=RAMkumar
Do you want to continue(1/0)? 1
press 1-compare 2-concatenate 3-length of string
enter your choice=3
enter string=ram **the length of string=3**
Do you want to continue(1/0)? 1

press 1-compare 2-concatenate 3-length of string enter your choice=4
wrong choice
Do you want to continue(1/0)? 0

Program 11: Develop a program to sort the given set of N numbers using Bubble sort.

```
#include<stdio.h>
int main()
{
int i,j,n,temp;
int a[20];
printf("enter the value of n");
scanf("%d",&n);
printf("Enter the numbers in unsorted order:\n");
for(i=0;i<n;i++)
scanf("%d", &a[i]);
```

- bubble sort logic for(i=0;i<n;i++)

```
{
for(j=0;j<(n-i)-1;j++)
{
if( a[j]>a[j+1])
{
temp=a[j];
a[j]=a[j+1];
a[j+1]=temp;
}
}
}
printf("The sorted array is\n");
for(i=0;i<n;i++)
{
printf("%d\n",a[i]);
}
}
```

Output

```
Enter the value of n
5
Enter the numbers one by one in unsorted order:
20
10
30
50
40
The sorted array is
10
20
30
40
```

50

Program 12: Develop a program to find the square root of a given number N and execute for all possible inputs with appropriate messages. Note: Don't use library function sqrt(n).

```
#include<stdio.h>
#include<math.h>
#include<stdlib.h>
int main()
{
int n;
float sqrt, temp;
printf("Enter a value whose square root has to be calculated\n");
scanf("%d",&n);
if(n<=0)
{
printf("Sqrt can't be determined");
exit(0);
}
sqrt = n / 2;
temp = 0;
while(sqrt != temp)
{
temp = sqrt;
sqrt = ( n/temp + temp) / 2;
}
printf("The square root of %d is %f", n, sqrt);
}
```

Output

Run1

Enter a value whose square root has to be calculated 9

The Square root of 9.000000=3.0000

Program 13: Implement structures to read, write, compute average- marks and the students scoring aboveand below the average marks for a class of N students.

```
#include<stdio.h>
struct student
{
char usn[10];
char name[10];
float m1,m2,m3;
float avg,total;
};
void main()
{
Struct student
S[20];
Int n,i;
float avg,sum=0.0;
printf("Enter the number of student=");
scanf("%d",&n);
```

```
for(i=0;i<n;i++)
{
printf("Enter the detail of %d students\n",i+1);
printf("\n Enter USN=");
scanf("%s",s[i].usn);
printf("\n Enter Name=");
scanf("%s",s[i].name);
printf("Enter the three subject score\n");
scanf("%f%f%f",&s[i].m1,&s[i].m2,&s[i].m3);
s[i].total=s[i].m1+s[i].m2+s[i].m3;
s[i].avg=s[i].total/3;
}
for(i=0;i<n;i++)
{
if(s[i].avg>=35)
printf("\n %s has scored above the average marks",s[i].name);
else
                                        printf("\n %s has scored below the average marks",s[i].name);
}
}
```

Output

Enter the number of student=2
Enter the detail of 1 students
Enter USN=101
Enter Name=john
Enter the three subject score 10 21 15
Enter the detail of 2 students
Enter USN=102
Enter Name=Kumar
Enter the three subject score 11 9 10
john has scored above the average marks
Kumar has scored below the average marks

Program 14: Develop a program using pointers to compute the sum, mean and standard deviation of allelements stored in an array of n real numbers.

```
#include<stdio.h>
#include<math.h>
int main()
{
int n , i;
float x[20],sum,mean;
float variance , deviation
printf("Enter the value of n \n");
scanf("%d",&n);
printf("enter %d real values \n",n);
for (i=0;i<n;i++)
{
scanf("%f",(x+i));
}
```

```
sum=0;
for(i=0;i<n;i++)
{
sum= sum+*(x+i);
}
printf("sum=%f\n",sum);
mean=sum/n;
sum=0;
for(i=0;i<n;i++)
{
sum=sum+(*(x+i)-mean)*(*(x+i)-mean);
}
variance=sum/n;
deviation=sqrt(variance);
printf("mean(Average)=%f\n",mean);
printf("variance=%f\n",variance);
printf("standard deviation=%f\n",deviation);
}
```

Output:

```
Entre the value of n
5
Enter 5 real values
3
7
23
1
4
sum=38.000000
mean(Average)=7.600000
variance=63.039997
standard deviation=7.939773
```

Program 15: Implement Recursive functions for Binary to Decimal Conversion.

```
#include <stdio.h>
#include <math.h>
int find(int x, int count)
{
if (x == 0)
return 0;
else
return(pow(2, count) * (x%10 ) + find(x/10 ,count+1));
}
void main()
{
int binary;
printf("Enter a Binary number:");
scanf ("%d",&binary);
printf(" The decimal value for binary %d is",binary);
printf("%d", find(binary,0));
```

```
}
```

Output: Enter a Binary number: 1010
The decimal value for binary 1010 is 10

Printed by Libri Plureos GmbH in Hamburg,
Germany